D1400100

DATE DUE

THE LIBRARY STORE   #47-0120

DEMCO

ACTING FOR CHILDREN

A PRIMER

Acting
for Children

A PRIMER

Mary Kane Lewis

The John Day Company

New York

19376

Copyright © 1969 by Mary Kane Lewis

All rights reserved. No part of this book may be reprinted, or reproduced or utilized in any form or by any electronic, mechanical or other means, now known or hereafter invented, including photocopying and recording, or in any information storage and retrieval system, without permission in writing from the Publisher, The John Day Company, Inc., 62 West 45th Street, New York, N.Y. 10036. Published on the same day in Canada by Longmans Canada Limited.

Library of Congress Catalogue Card Number: 69-10814

PRINTED IN THE UNITED STATES OF AMERICA

For my husband,
Mark Lewis

Introduction

This is a book about teaching acting to children. For many years I have been holding drama classes at the Pittsburgh Playhouse for children, teen-agers, young adults and adults (both at the avocational and professional levels) and at various schools, clubs, and colleges in the community.

This particular class with the beginning eight- to twelve-year-olds has been held weekly, in a theatrical setting, away from the regular school. There is a modest fee attached. It is a class that could be taught in a club, community center, drama school, or in any grade school.

No matter where it is held, I would recommend that only interested, enthusiastic children be permitted to enroll. Grades or IQ's should have nothing to do with it. Bright children find drama great fun and are usually very good at it; but very often children who have appeared colorless and dull, through drama begin to reveal very vivid personality traits that were heretofore hidden. It goes without saying that the child must be mature enough to realize the subtle formality of the actor-audience relationship. Of course, whom the teacher chooses to accept in her class for special reasons is her own concern.

While an undergraduate in the Department of Drama in the

Fine Arts College of Carnegie Institute of Technology (now Carnegie-Mellon University), I majored in acting and teaching. Further graduate study in the Speech Department at the University of Pittsburgh found me also appearing in productions at the Pittsburgh Playhouse. This simultaneous interest continued through the years. Graduate work at Pitt included the study of Creative Dramatics, which I later taught at that institution for a year. This is to say that although I understand creative dramatics and appreciate its theories and techniques, this is not a book about creative dramatics.

Rather it is a book that approaches acting as an art form. Like painting, music, and the dance, the creativity in the art of acting is manifested through form and technique. Acting is an old art, a noble art, and through the study of it in this fashion, we develop a deeper appreciation and respect for the art that it is.

All intelligent children who like drama, whether they be talented to a degree or not, gain immeasurably from it. In drama class a child begins to feel an awareness of himself, his physical presence. The study of people in dramatic situations intensifies into an appreciation for the depiction of life through the art form known as theater, and later, into a genuine love for this form of art. I like to think that we can help him most if we succeed in building an acute awareness of self and others into a permanent and lively interest in all human beings and the various structures and complications that constitute life.

MARY KANE LEWIS

Contents

Part I: GETTING STARTED

LESSON 1. Initiation   13

LESSON 2. An Actor Is Special   20

Part II: IMPROVISING

LESSON 3. Improvising with Three Characters   28

LESSON 4. Improvising with Two Characters   38

LESSON 5. Improvisations with One Character   49

Part III: ATTENDING TO OUR SPEECH

LESSON 6. Articulation and Expression   57

LESSON 7. Articulation and Pronunciation   63

LESSON 8. Articulation and the Script   68

LESSON 9. Articulation and Movement   71

Part IV: MIMING AND MUSIC

LESSON 10. Explaining the Assignment   75

LESSON 11. Discussing Each Selection   79

LESSON 12. Completing Our Ideas   85

LESSON 13. Setting Our Business   89

LESSON 14. Polishing Our Pantomimes   93

LESSON 15. Last-Minute Pointers   95

LESSON 16. Performance of Musical Pantomime   98

Part V: EXPLORING THE STAGE

LESSON 17. A Bit About the Stage   101

LESSON 18. Stage Areas and Body Positions   106

LESSON 19. Review and Other Techniques   110

LESSON 20. Students Give Directions   114

LESSON 21. Review with Pantomime   117

Part VI: HANDLING THE SCRIPT

LESSON 22. Reading and Blocking   119

LESSON 23. Making Sure   125

LESSON 24. We Play the Scene   128

Part VII: PREPARING THE PLAY

LESSON 25. Reading and Casting   130

LESSON 26. Blocking and Script Marking   134

LESSON 27. Lines and Cues   137

LESSON 28. Costumes and Props   139

LESSON 29. Character Development   144

LESSON 30. Imagination and Character   148

LESSON 31. Dress Rehearsal 152

LESSON 32. Performance 154

PLAYLETS FOR STUDY

Coffee 156

Dream Dust for Shadows 159

The Secret of the Old Cave 165

Another Day 168

Once in a Blue Moon 172

PART I

Getting Started

Initiation

The stage—enchanting, mysterious, a world of shadows and dreams. Through the ages, it is here that man has come to be inspired, innervated, released. Small wonder, then, that it is the ideal place for the child—curious, enthusiastic, and full of the spirit of Let's Pretend—to find himself!

A Playing Space

Every child has special qualities, uniquely his own, which need expression. Naturally, the amounts of enthusiasm and creativity he brings to drama class have the most to do with his successfully projecting his character across the footlights. However, the physical aspects of the playing space are also of utmost importance.

For beginners like the eight- to twelve-year-olds we are concerned with here, I prefer a small room with an elevated platform which is easily accessible to both student and teacher. Under these conditions it is possible to introduce new points or practice movements and gestures onstage, thus maintaining the atmosphere of the theater at all times. Unfortunately, the teacher might be assigned a room with no platform. If she has access to some funds, it is a simple matter to rig up a curtain.

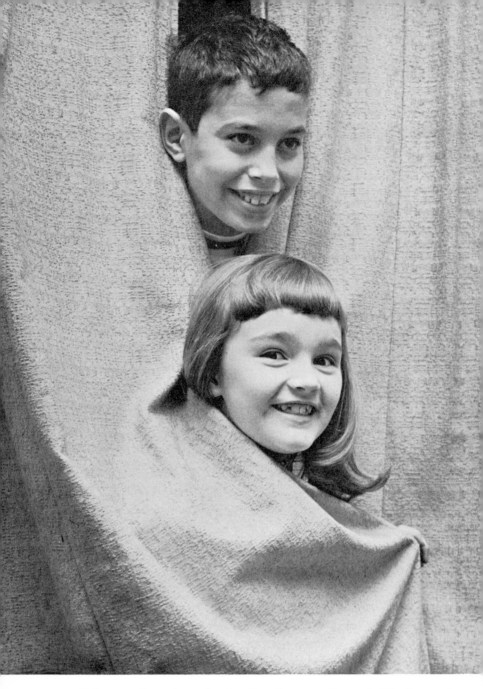

"We are all ready to begin. Our lines are learned. We know the action. Now we are waiting for our audience. Isn't it fun to be an actor?"

Even better, a carpenter can build a small stage at minimal cost.

Whatever the means of creating it, a feeling of separation from the audience enhances the dramatic mood and the sense of his own specialness which the young player needs to spin his web of enchantment. It also strikes his fancy to think of it as a constantly moving picture within a frame called a *proscenium arch.*

This is really an old Greek word, but it is a new word for us. It means to be in front of the scene. *Pro skene. Pro*, meaning in front of; *skene*, meaning scene. So you see, the arch is in front of the scene, framing it. And remember, the people who come to watch, to view this picture that is constantly moving, are the audience. They are very important. They want to see healthy, handsome people moving gracefully, speaking clearly, and acting truthfully. What do you think this means—to act truthfully? Who would like to tell us? (*Hands go up. We discuss here.*) Yes, people like to watch what they see around them every day acted out on a stage, sometimes exaggerated and made more exciting. They have liked this from the earliest days. This is why we have actors and audiences and stages.

Loosening Up

Both teacher and pupil need time to get acquainted and appraise each other. The child should be allowed to relax, look around, and absorb the new atmosphere. The teacher should take this opportunity to observe the child and find out *why* he has come to drama class.

One easy relaxer is to generate a discussion and let the class take part in it. "Who do you think was the first actor?" "Didn't the Indians wear makeup?" "Why was the witch doctor so different from the rest of the tribe?" "Who were the early Greeks? Their theater was something like our football stadium, wasn't it?" Such a discussion quickly stimulates these young actors and relaxes them for their first assignment in class—a self-introduction. Such talk should also provide the background for their first prepared assignment before the next lesson—a two to three minute talk about some subject directly concerned with theater, the stage, or acting.

Teacher Is a Kind of Actor

It is the teacher who must create the casual, relaxed atmosphere for the first introductions. As she stands in front of the group at Downstage Center, a spot which she has designated for the introductions to take place, she begins:

Here I am, boys and girls, at Downstage Center, a good place to get attention—down near the audience, right at the center. Think for a moment that I am someone special, set aside from the rest of you. This is what is so special about being an actor. He stands in front of a group who watches and listens. But he must be lively, entertaining, and interesting to watch.

If I am a witch, I may look like this—menacing, cruel, mysterious, and evil. (*The teacher becomes a good, convincing witch.*) If I am a clown, I am entirely different. Sad, one minute. Happy, the next. (*Again a demonstration.*) Whatever I am doing—being frightening or funny, moving excitedly, or quietly talking—whatever it is I am doing, I am away from the group, set apart, someone special. People are watching and listening, and they wish to be interested, pleased, entertained. If I am enthusiastic to tell people such a simple thing as my name and where I live, people will listen, because they feel my enthusiasm.

As an actor, when I stand like this on the stage in front of others, I must be very relaxed, unafraid, brave. Nothing must frighten or embarrass me. Here I can do anything, be anything— a fierce pirate or a wiggly mermaid. How powerful I am! How special! I can frighten people, make them laugh or cry. But I must be calm, relaxed, and poised all the while I am doing this, so that I do not make them uneasy. What do these words mean? (*Hands go up. We talk.*)

Ideas of action and adventure naturally appeal to boys. Sometimes a visit to a bigger stage where we find bigger props inspires us with 'bigger ideas.'

Also I must speak clearly and deliberately so that they will understand everything I have to say. I must be *confident.* Confidence is a very good thing for an actor to have. If he is confident, he is relaxed—speaks well, moves easily. Who wants to tell us more about confidence? (*More hands. We discuss.*)

Now, are we ready to tell the class something about ourselves? Something simple, perhaps? About our family, our neighbors? What interests us? Why have we come to drama class?

Remember, we are going to be actors. We must get to know one another well—and soon—so that we can work together in a relaxed fashion. If you are anxious to tell us something about yourself, we will be eager to listen. It is a contagious thing, like the measles! Ready? Good! Who would like to be first?

A Good Beginning

This is an initiation lesson. The children are initiated to their teacher, the subject, their surroundings, and one another. Time is of the essence. We do not have a week to get acquainted, only an hour or so. The teacher should be very good at names, learning them as quickly as possible. Everytime she stands in front of the class at Downstage Center, she does so consciously, stimulating them to get up and take her place. A bit of comedy or tragedy helps here. The little players should want to get up and take over.

As each child gets up to tell about himself it may be necessary to prod a little. Invent questions pertinent to his talk if he seems to have little to say. "How many brothers and sisters do you have?" "What kind of plays do you like best?" "What kind of plays do they give in school?" During this first lesson the teacher should convince these beginners that she is their comrade and fellow actor, as well as being the captain of their ship, *New Adventure,* which is just about to leave port for exciting sailing!

The following is a suggested lesson sheet which the teacher may give to the students at the beginning of each lesson. It is a good idea either to read it with the children at the beginning of class or to call upon several children to read each point aloud. If the teacher chooses not to distribute the lesson sheet, it will serve as a directive to her, keeping the class within bounds of the material to be covered. I have found such a sheet valuable, too, for parents, for it gives them an accurate record of what the child is accomplishing at each lesson.

Lesson 1

1. The first thing you will learn in drama class today is the name of your new teacher.
2. After you and your teacher talk a little about acting, the theater, and the stage, she will ask you to give a short talk about yourself to the rest of the class.
3. Come to Downstage Center. Stand very straight; think yourself tall; and speak very clearly.
4. Talking to a group can be fun. Enjoy yourself. Relax. Smile and look happy.
5. Tell your audience your name (nickname if you prefer), your age, where you live, attend school. If you have a hobby you enjoy, mention it. Include something interesting that has happened in your life lately: a trip you took, a person you met, something that occurred in the neighborhood.
6. The reason we want you to give this introduction well is because it is very important for every actor to begin his training by learning to speak with CONFIDENCE and POISE. Today you will discuss these words and what they mean. Whether you are an actor or not, it is important to speak clearly so that everyone can understand you.
7. Be sure to learn your teacher's name and those of your new friends.

Assignment for next lesson:

Prepare a short talk between two and three minutes long on something in the theater that interests you. Perhaps you would like to talk a little more about something we discussed today. Here are a few suggestions:

Why I Like to Act
Indian Makeup
An Indian Witch Doctor
My Favorite Actor
The First Actor
Actors Are Special
My Favorite TV Show
A Play I Saw
Puppets
A Big Arena—the First Stage

LESSON 2

An Actor Is Special

During the second lesson the drama teacher continues to stress the specialness and separateness of the actor. She reminds the class that the first actors were people who had something special to say to the rest of the tribe. To do this they usually stood in a place apart, sometimes on an elevation. They readied their bodies and their voices to make this special announcement.

Enjoy Yourselves

This is an important day. Everyone has prepared his talk and sits ready to be called upon. The teacher begins by telling the children how enjoyable class is going to be today:

All of you have spent considerable time preparing to tell us something about the theater, and we are all ready and eager to listen. Here we sit, while you, Albert or Kathleen, go to a special place and tell us what you have been waiting to say. Remember, each speaker is very important today, and he has in his power the ability to be king of his special place onstage, his own little world. When he comes to Downstage Center to talk to us, he must feel that he is able to do anything.

Here the teacher can close her eyes, stretch out both arms, and turn around and around. If she is agile, she can raise one foot high and hop on the other. She does this a few times to let the children see that she does not mind looking ludicrous. She hopes to transmit this lack of fear or embarrassment to the class. If they see her, a grown-up, jumping around like this, fear leaves them, too.

Anything—anything and everything is what the king or queen should be able to do onstage. This is his world, and he must be relaxed in it, the master of it. Let's think for a moment about the Red Queen in *Alice in Wonderland*, shall we? Here was a queen who seemed crazy to Alice. Easily as mad as the Hatter! Yet, she does the craziest things with a great deal of authority, simply because she feels she is the boss. Today as you give your talks try to feel a little like a king or queen. In fact, you are going to be one or two jumps ahead of the Red Queen, because what you are going to say will make some sense.

How We Should Stand

At this point the teacher can ask the students to think about the people they have seen give talks in school and who did not stand the right way. "How did they stand? What was poor about their posture? What did the teacher say to them? Who would like to show us?" The hands go up so fast it is difficult to select one, because we are on familiar territory now. It is

"How good it feels to stand here on the stage in front of the curtain! How special! By the way, let me introduce myself. My name is _____."

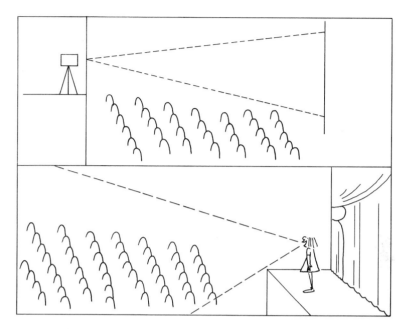

good to have several demonstrations of poor speakers. "Now who would like to show us a good way to stand? Ah, yes, that is quite nice."

How We Should Talk

Here the teacher can repeat what she just did in regard to posture. Having the class recreate their own impressions of children who whisper or talk through clenched jaws with bowed heads brings the point home all the stronger.

At this time, too, the teacher can talk about the word *projection* and explain its meaning. She can compare the projection of the voice to that of a moving picture projector in the projection booth of a theater, whose job it is to project a bigger image on the screen. If she has access to a blackboard, a diagram will help. However, most children today are familiar with slides and home movies and easily grasp the meaning. It is important that they be made to realize that there is a process to making the voice bigger, but that it takes time and work to accomplish this.

Then, too, we must use very careful speech today. Let's sound our *t*'s and strengthen our *b*'s. For, after all, this is only good manners, isn't it? People are gathered together to listen to us, and we must courteously try to please them with speech they can understand and appreciate.

Now, are we ready to give our talks? Remember to look lively and be interested in what you have to say. If you are enthusiastic, so will we be. We are excited to hear what you have to say, eager to have you begin.

As the children give their talks it is a good idea for the teacher to keep paper and pencil handy and jot down things she wants to comment upon when all are finished. I generally emphasize all the good points at this lesson, giving individual praise for the smallest thing that seemed well done. If the teacher asks, "Children, what did you notice about the talks that we can improve?" she will find many raising their hands, eager to criticize. Certainly, she must take these points into consideration, because the children have noticed things that were obviously poor. Criticism is a very healthy and necessary part of the teaching and learning of drama. Children find it fun to discover mistakes, so they watch keenly. As we progress with each lesson we find there is a right and wrong way to do everything. One of the great advantages in taking a class in drama, if it is taught correctly, lies in the fact that, as in ballet or physical education, a discipline is established. But the teacher should be careful that the criticisms do not get out of hand.

Of course, if the class is large (twelve or more), the comments will have to be kept at a minimum and can be treated in a general way. The teacher can always smooth over an opinion that seems too salty, such as "She kept her eyes on the floor, and I couldn't hear her." "Well, that is true," the teacher replies, "but did you notice the beautifully soft voice Marilyn has to work with, once she starts letting it come out bigger and fuller?" The teacher may also find that, with a small class that is slow getting started, she will have to prod with a few questions, perhaps even illustrate with a story herself. This helps relax them in the early lessons. If there is time at the end of the period, she may have further demonstrations of posture and voice from each child.

These primary lessons are specially contrived so that the teacher will have time to search deeply into the faces of the children before her. She will find some eager to communicate, others reticent. The latter deserve extra attention, especially at the beginning. Since time is short in a class of this type, it is urgent that they be made to feel very relaxed with the teacher and a part of the group. Very often the shy, quiet child is extremely imaginative and has been playing for years in his own little dreamworld, which he is not anxious to disturb with playmates. It is up to the teacher to bring him out of his shell. She can start by including him in the discussions at once, asking him questions, looking for his opinions often. Serious, wry at times, but quick to perceive humor, usually he begins to open up during the improvisations.

The Next Step—Improvisations

As the teacher winds up the second lesson she reminds the class that they are going to be doing something entirely different at Lesson 3.

Next time we will be doing *improvisations.* A big word, isn't it? To improvise means to act, or do something, on the spur of the moment. This will be easy for you. You do it everytime you pretend. Well, that's what we will be doing at the next lesson.

In a sense, we will be pretending. And I want you to bring in some good ideas for us to act out. Suppose each of you brings in two ideas. Each idea must have *three* people in it, and these three people must be involved in a dramatic situation that will be easy for us to act out. For instance, a mother and a daughter disagree over whether the daughter should be allowed to stay up to watch a certain TV program. The father overhears and gives his opinion.

Each idea must include a beginning, middle, and end. This is the cornerstone of all good plays. We must find ideas that take place in one locale, preferably one room, so that we can stick to the point. The idea must have a good dramatic situation in it. It may even have a *conflict* in it, another ingredient for a good play. Conflict means that there is some disagreement in your idea. The characters may disagree with one another or fight against a situation. Good plays are like good cakes. They need sugar and spice to make them interesting. Do you understand what we are going to do? Are there any questions?

And so the pupils leave class at this lesson with something to ponder on. For the next few lessons they will become deeply immersed in the dramatic situation. Daily occurrences will take on a dramatic tone for them. Next week they will begin to act, and we shall see what we shall see!

Lesson 2

1. Today you are going to give a two to three minute talk on something that interests you.
2. Remember, in order for people to be interested in what you have to say, they must understand you.
3. Pronounce your words carefully. Don't be afraid to use your lips and tongue. These are very important for good, clear speech.
4. Stand straight and tall. No one enjoys looking at Sam Slouch or Sally Swayback! Before you start to give your speeches we will talk about good posture.

5. Relax, and have fun! Enjoy telling us about something in the theater, and we will enjoy listening.
6. Be interested in what you have to say. If you are interested, your listeners will be, too.
7. Talk loud enough so that everyone will hear you. This is what actors call PROJECTION. Making the voice bigger.
8. Remember, don't rush. Take it easy. Don't drag your words, but talk slowly enough for everyone to understand you.

Assignment for next lesson:

Next week we are going to start to ACT, or make believe. Every one knows how to make believe, or pretend. This is what acting is. We will start to learn to act by doing a series of exercises called improvisations. Your teacher will explain this word. In order to do improvisations, we must have good ideas to work with. So you are to put your name on a piece of paper, write down two ideas for THREE people to act out, and give this paper to your teacher next week. Each idea must contain an interesting dramatic situation, with a good beginning, middle, and end. Your ideas may be humorous or serious. In fact, one or two of your characters may disagree with the other, or others, to provide conflict.

PART II

Improvising

LESSON 3

Improvising with Three Characters

Today we are going to do improvisations. There is excitement in the air as the children start coming into class. We check the roll by having each child answer with a word, words, or a phrase that requires careful pronunciation, like wash (not worsh), wouldn't you (not woon't choo), or Close the clothes closet. Doing this begins to awaken in them a feeling for articulation and careful speech. We repeat this roll-calling procedure at every lesson.

Let's Pretend

After the roll has been checked, the teacher collects the ideas for the improvisations. She can begin by starting to read them aloud.

"Here are Mary Sue's ideas. As I read them try to think which idea will be the best for us to act out.

1. Two sisters are in the kitchen. They are arguing about who will wash the dishes, who will dry. Their mother comes in and settles the argument.

2. Three girls are walking home from school. They are going to have a party. One wants to have boys. One wants girls. The other doesn't care."

The hands go up. Chances are the second idea is going to have the greater appeal because of the boy-girl-party theme. But this idea goes nowhere. It provides conversation. That's all.

"But wait a moment! What did we say were the three basic ingredients for a good improvisation? Claudia?"

Claudia responds vigorously, "A beginning, middle, and end."

"Good! What else? Jim?"

"They should take place in one place, and they should have a conflict," says Jim.

"Right! A conflict means that one thing is working against another. It doesn't necessarily mean that there is always fighting going on. We know that Snow White was good. Now who or what was she in conflict with?"

There is no doubt in Suellen's mind. "The wicked queen."

"Correct. So we see here that even though Snow White does not fight, is not quarrelsome, we know a conflict is taking place between the forces of good and evil. A conflict makes the scene more interesting. It gives the characters more interesting things to do and be."

As the children absorb this, the teacher refers back to the improvisation they originally started to discuss.

"Now which of Mary Sue's ideas seems to have the best beginning, middle, and end within it; and which seems to have the best locale, the best scene?"

They think for a few moments. Louis is ready. "I guess the first." Margie is next. "But I like the party one best." Scott says, "I don't like none of them. Where are the boys in it?"

The teacher intervenes: "Of course, boys are very necessary for a good scene. But as I leaf through the other ideas I see plenty of chances for you boys. Besides, you know, there are plays for all boys and plays for all girls. These are for special schools, camps, and clubs. But now let's try to decide why the first idea is the best one to choose."

Anne makes the discovery. "I think it has a better start and end. The girls are in the kitchen doing something, and when their mother comes in and brings an end to the argument and tells them what she wants to do—that is the end."

Teacher agrees. "Yes. Mother always has the last word. That's final. Right?"

Then they all agree, so we cast this scene and play it.

Three's a Crowd

Many of the ideas for the first improvisations go nowhere. The teacher must expect this. First of all, three is an odd number. It's easier to find ideas for two. But improvisations with three play well once they get going. By incorporating three into the first improvisations, the burden of dialogue is lessened; three people are tossing the ball, not two. The shy little introverts don't have too much to say with an extrovert carrying the ball, but they do manage to say something. This is at least a beginning. It becomes obvious at once who will dominate the scene, who will not. But this is not bad. The seeds of courage are being planted.

It takes thought and discussion before most of the children really understand what a good idea is. "Three girls decide to have a slumber party" goes nowhere. We quickly dismiss themes like these, if we can, because previous experiment has proved that they all would end up as just talk. With an idea like this one: "Two boy scouts and a saleslady. The saleslady tries to sell them an electric appliance," we have to prod. Vague as it seemed at first, later familiarity with the ten-year-old boy who submitted it revealed an imagination obsessed with details about boy scout camping and every conceivable object of camping equipment there is. His mind skipped quickly from

In this scene we learn to talk and listen as well as handle 'props'
which are sometimes difficult. Having a tea party is a good improv-
isation idea for three people.

one point to another, and he brought in as many as ten props for a musical pantomime. With ideas like this that have a good germ of action in them, we have to give the three players plenty of time to decide just what sort of action they can carry through with.

The children begin to see more clearly as we do more improvisations and discuss them. Some possess dramatic instinct from the start. Here are two ideas submitted by a talented ten-year-old girl:

1. The New Shoes

CHARACTERS: a girl about eleven, a mother, a shoe store clerk

The girl is trying on shoes in a store. She goes through ten pairs of shoes all selected by her mother. Finally, the shoe clerk brings a pair of high heeled boots with yellow and red polka dots and green stripes. "Perfect" said the girl and puts on the shoes. A mother and daughter argument follows in which no one wins. "Oh, skip it," says the mother, "you can wear your dirty old tennis shoes." And they left the store.

2. The Red Paint

CHARACTERS: a cleaning lady, a mother, a girl about eight

The mother leaves the house leaving the cleaning lady in charge. The little girl pleads with the cleaning lady to let her paint the swing set. The kind hearted cleaning lady agrees. *But* when she looks out the window about 5 minutes later and sees the girl and the swing set well painted she rushes out and grabs the little girl and gives her a frantic scrubbing. When the mother comes home she notices a red spot on the girl's hair, but knowing the kind hearted cleaning lady, and the little girl's talent for making messes, she just winks and doesn't say a word.

Both of these scenes reveal a feeling for character and the dramatic situation, along with a sense of timing.

As improvisations continue the teacher always gives each

cast a few minutes to discuss the scene with one another. They talk over what they are going to do. They arrange the furniture properly and attempt to keep the action on the track.

"Remember, your ideas must begin, go somewhere, and then end," the teacher reminds them.

As the children enact these first improvisations, the two things they find most difficult are keeping within the framework of the original idea and timing it well. Very often they take the action on- and offstage repeatedly. One person is usually at fault for this. In some cases the teacher will have to interrupt and make a suggestion that will bring it to an end.

More often than not, she will be amazed at the feeling for proportion and good common sense these children possess. At this age they are keen observers of life. In many cases they come up with an almost perfect script, complete with gags and timing. "Hi, cupcake! Is dinner ready yet?" the scene begins. Then she tells him about a new hat she just put on the charge account, and the sponsors of the new TV comedy show have stiff competition.

Getting them to think of ideas and problem situations concerning discipline is good, too. They are familiar with them and try to solve them. Obedience and disobedience in the home and school is a good theme:

1. A teacher asks the mother to come and discuss the child who is doing poorly in school. Why? They call the child in.
2. Mother tells father that John has been bad. Father and John discuss it.

Situations of humor are most popular. Children have a field day with ideas of this sort:

1. A dentist; reluctant child; mother.
2. A doctor giving a shot; the child; the mother.

3. Grandma takes Junior's part. What does Mom do?
4. Mother and father try to talk daughter out of getting her ears pierced.
5. Younger sister and brother console big sister who hasn't yet been invited to the Spring Frolic dance.

By having the children think about situations for improvisations, the teacher is introducing them to *plot*. She can tell the children that plot is an outline, or general plan, of the action of the story. With certain classes of eleven- and twelve-year-olds, she may go into more detail about plot if she wishes. Our simple beginning, middle, and end is fairly comparable to rising action, falling action, climax, and conclusion. They can certainly understand character and setting. But in our case plot is almost always an episode or an incident.

Example

PLACE: Shoe store.
ACTORS: Shoe salesman, preferably hippy.
   Teen-age girl
   Her very old-fashioned old grandmother.
PLOT: The grandmother is taking the granddaughter to the shoe store to get whatever she (granddaughter) wants. Unfortunately, what she wants is high boots.

Example

PLACE: At home
ACTORS: Father
   Mother (sweet type)
   Teen-age son
PLOT: The son has just rammed up the family's new car.

Here is one from a naturally talented boy whose hair was constantly falling in his eyes: "Father, housewife, boy—deciding whether or not the boy should get his hair cut—in a living room."

Here is another nicely self-contained incident: The scene is a candy counter. There is a nice saleslady and a crabby saleslady. A little kid comes along who doesn't know the first thing about money. The nice saleslady wants to give him candy for free, but the other one says, "NO." The nice saleslady gives him some when the other isn't looking.

Boys are very involved with medicine, science, and science fiction these days. Their ideas roam the universe. At this age they are also brimming with adventure. Their ideas spill over with it:

1. Two boys are in a haunted house. They meet a ghost.
2. Two robbers in a bank cracking a safe. The policeman comes.

I like to postpone scenes like these until the end of class. There is usually much noise, excitement, many entrances and exits. The teacher should try to include the quiet, reticent boys in these improvisations. The free-for-all raucousness usually relieves their tension. But once the peace has been disturbed, it is difficult to recapture it.

The teacher should give the more outgoing members of the class a chance to play together at least once during the first improvisations. By this time she has a fairly good idea who they are. They leave the class with a sense of satisfaction if given the opportunity to work with someone of equal volubility.

Why We Improvise

On a higher level, improvisations are used continually in drama classes. They enable professional actors to renew their imaginative resources and refresh their acting skills. Something akin to them is employed by psychiatrists in their search to aid emotionally disturbed patients. In psychology we find role-playing teams experimenting with improvisational techniques that will bring better success to personnel training methods in business and industry.

For eight- to twelve-year-olds, improvisations are exhilarating fun. They provide release for all the pent-up perceptions they have accumulated over the years. Since they choose their own material, they are on very familiar ground. They have only recently left the world of make-believe and feel very much at home. I find them invaluable for the teacher, especially at the beginning, because they very soon tell her everything she wants to know about the child. If she feels a certain child can be brought out of a shell by doing a specific type of improvisation, they can create it immediately in class.

For instance, if she senses that one tall, thin, awkward girl already feels uncomfortable beside the other, more petite, twelve-year-olds, she can choose such a simple idea as the Cinderella theme. She suggests the scene where Cinderella helps the stepsisters get ready for the ball. She asks this girl to play Cinderella and casts two others as the stepsisters. After they have done it once the class discusses it. The teacher is careful to call attention to what a good Cinderella they had and why. Then she suggests that they do it again, changing parts so that our plain Jane has a chance to play one of the witchy stepsisters. By this time she is beginning to feel at home. If there is time before the class ends, perhaps this girl can play Cinderella again, this time after she has been transformed into a glamorous beauty by the Fairy Godmother. Such an approach usually works wonders very quickly. Although it takes a while for this type of youngster to become downright loquacious, concentrating on changing roles quickly like this forces her to use resources she didn't know she possessed.

Before class ends the teacher prepares the children for their assignment—another improvisation. She asks each one to bring in two ideas for two people to act out.

Remember, it is *two* people we are interested in this time. Be sure to think of ideas that give two people plenty of incentive to do something together and talk. We call conversation between two people on stage a *dialogue*. This is a word that applies to all conversation in plays. Have you ever heard this word used by anyone? How?

As they leave, the teacher adds one final reminder—to pay particular attention to situations with two people until the class meets again.

"You will be surprised how interesting things will become that you didn't notice before!"

Lesson 3

1. Today is your first acting day.
2. This is the day you do your first improvisation. A new word for you, IMPROVISATION. It means to make something up on the spur of the moment. But you have to have the idea first.
3. In this exercise today you are going to improvise, or make something up. We will use the ideas you have brought with you to class.
4. When you do an improvisation, it is your first step in acting. You must use your imagination, or pretend. Your mind invents things for you to pretend to do. If three people are going to pretend to be on a picnic, they must try to do all the things that people on picnics do. Eat, drink, play ball, etc. When we improvise, we try to feel just the same as we do when we are doing these things in real life.
5. In this exercise we must talk, laugh, move, and sound like real people in real life. In improvising we do something on the spur of the moment, then it is over, forgotten about forever unless we try to do the same thing again. But our words will not be

exactly the same a second time, because we do not have a script. With a script, we memorize words. When we improvise, we don't learn words.

6. So if we pretend that we are on a picnic, we must THINK that we are on a picnic, FEEL that we are on a picnic, and do all the things that we would do on a picnic.

7. When you do this improvisation today, try to make it as much like real life as possible—just as you would do the scene if you were really living it.

8. As an actor, you should begin to observe closely the actions of people and try to imitate their actions as closely as possible.

Assignment for next lesson:

Next week we are going to do improvisations with TWO people, and we will need many good ideas for two people to act out. So write your name on a piece of paper and jot down two good ideas for two people to act out.

LESSON 4

Improvising with Two Characters

The teacher collects the ideas for improvisations with two people. She knows that they will present a greater challenge than those in Lesson 3. First of all, two people, not three, share the burden of dialogue. These improvisations will require greater concentration.

Let's Concentrate

Concentration! What is concentration? (*Hands go up. We discuss.*) Think for a moment, boys and girls, of your math class in school. All of a sudden your teacher says, "Pay close attention everyone. We are going to do a little addition." And almost before you can shake off your brain dust, she rolls off a list of figures expecting you to come up with the right answer immediately, doesn't she? Finding the correct sum of these figures requires concentration, doesn't it? Part of concentration is listening, too—and thinking. If you didn't listen and think as she rattles off the numbers, you couldn't add.

So listening and thinking add up to concentration, which is very important to improvising and acting. Improvisations demand good concentration. We hope that if you concentrate well, you will produce good dialogue—dialogue that shows you have been listening and thinking. At the close of the last lesson we mentioned that dialogue is a name we give to all types of conversation in plays. When the characters in the play speak to one another or to a god or an object or to the audience, this is what we call dialogue. The playwright, the man who creates the play, writes the dialogue. So today you become playwrights as well as actors when you improvise and write your own dialogue.

Ideas to Work With

The teacher starts to look over the ideas. What a variety they present! Quickly scanning them, she knows which will play well, which will not. Some are carelessly submitted. Others bear the stamp of painful labor. Sometimes ideas which are very dramatic need to be channeled a little. It is well to scan them quickly, without mentioning them aloud until she has made a choice. The teacher should always have several good ideas of her own on hand, just in case we have a bad day. This is unlikely, but it does happen. She can use a better idea without mentioning names. Some ideas will be excellent, others unworkable. The latter is due to several factors. Sometimes the children haven't really grasped the idea or are getting lost in minor details or are searching for the dramatic in a really uneventful situation. Since time is usually short, it is best not to experiment with ideas we know are not workable. The children will learn best what we want by doing improvisations one after the other. There is rarely enough time to use everyone's idea, anyway.

We give these assignments so that the children will begin to observe around them, in the periphery of their own experience. It goes without saying that good ideas deserve attention and notice. I always credit the child aloud for submitting a workable idea. If an idea has to be padded a little, we are careful to explain why we are making the addition or the change. The teacher should expect to give more help to the eight- and nine-year-olds than to the older children. Sometimes a demonstration is a good thing to start off with. The teacher may play the mother. She may select a boy or girl from the class to play with her. They may choose a simple idea, like "You are being punished this afternoon because you didn't make your bed this morning and straighten up your room. Why?"

Duologues with Dialogue

Here are three ideas from a mature ten-year-old:

1. A brother and sister are arguing over which TV program to watch. Then they find out neither program is on because of a news special, so they go outside to play.

2. A girl is trying to remind her forgetful friend that today is her birthday, without coming right out and saying it. It turns out that her friend knew all the time but wanted to surprise her with a present.

3. There is one piece of candy left. The two girls are both trying to be polite by giving the piece to each other when each one really wants it. While they're trying to give it

to each other the candy drops to the ground and that is that.

Sharon, also ten years old, submitted these:
1. A girl is baby-sitting. She has to put a hard-to-manage child to bed who does not want to go.
2. A boy is late for dinner. He crept into the house, but his mother caught him. He tries to make excuses but his mother will not believe him.
3. A girl is trying to coax her mother that she needs a new dress for a party. When her mother knows her old party dress will do.

Ten-year-old Cheryl's imagination takes a different turn:

1. The Other Half

Two girls have to share the same Social Studies book. They both complain about the other person having the better side of the book. Finally they rip it in half and still complain. Finally they trade sides of the book and see that the other half is not as good as they thought. So they get a new Social Studies book and try again.

2. Friends to the End

Two boys were arguing over something. At first they argued vocally. Soon it turned into a fist fight. And just as one boy was about to get punched in the stomach he asked what they'd been arguing about, the other boy didn't know so they forgot about the fight and walked off "friends to the end!"

3. The New Boy

A girl is asked to show a new boy around the school. When she is showing him the playground she slipped and sprained her ankle and cannot walk. He has a horrible time trying to find the nurse's office. When he does she has gone out for a coffee break. Finally he finds the janitor and he works everything out okay!

Here are three ideas from a very good little actress, ten years old:

1. Trying to Sell a Car

There was a man who was trying to sell a secondhand car. The car looked like a fifth hand car. No one would buy it until one day a dum teenager walked in, and admired nothing else but this car.

2. The Kid Nextdoor

The girl next door is threeteen and the other girl was ten. The threeteen year old girl's name was Beth the other girls name was Mary. Beth was very mean to the other girls, but most of all. Beth picked on Mary.

3. My Danceing Bear

One day my pink teddy Bear started to dance. I was just about to go to sleep when my Teddy Bear started to dance.

These ideas belong to a ten-year-old boy who was enrolled in the class because his imagination spilled over into storytelling at home. He began to invent things:

1. A boy was practicing baseball and he threw the ball up and hit it with the bat. And the ball went really high and broke a window. Then an old lady came out and saw the boy. Then she ask him if he did it and the boy said yes. Then he said that he would buy a new one and fix it. Then the old lady said thank you.

2. A brother and sister were fighting over a football ticket And then the brother remebered that he had enough money to buy a football ticket. And then they went to the football game together.

3. A boy was walking along the street and he saw a boy cross the street and car was coming real fast and then the other boy ran across real fast and grab the boy. The boy was grateful for what the other boy had done. And then he gave him 1 dollar.

Here is an example of a ten-year-old's involvement with detail:

2 Girls

Part I

Two city girls went on a trip to a farm. They got in a lot of trouble and had plenty of problems. First they fed the chickens when they fed them. Then one of them fell into a pig pen Then the other one fell over a fence and ripped her pants.

Part II

Then their aunt asked them to go to the mailbox and get the mail. On the way to the mail box saw a meadow full of wild flowers and they stopped to pick some so they picked and picked till they got so tired they laid down in the meadow and went to sleep.

Part III

A couple hours later they woke up and grab their flowers and they run down to get the male. But someone had already got the mail. So they ran to the house and tried to explain

but their aunt packed them up and sent them back to the
city.

The ideas of the beginning twelve-year-olds take on a different maturity. They reveal new concerns growing from keener
observations of adult situations and their relationships with
adults:

1. Two girls get their own apartment and they dont' keep
   house very well. Mother calls and says she's coming to
   see their new apartment. The place is a shambles and
   Mom's very fussy so they rush to clean up.
2. Two girls are alone in the house at night. They are afraid.
3. A girl has no boyfriend and is jealous of her girlfriend's
   boyfriend. She invents a dream boy. Over the phone she
   tells her girl friend he is visiting her. Surprise! The girlfriend comes to see what he looks like. What does she
   do? What does she say?

These ideas belong to a very serious twelve-year-old:

1. A father and daughter who disagree on their choices of
   music. He likes classical and she likes rock 'n' roll. He
   complains that it's too loud and they argue.
2. A busy store clerk is impatient because a customer
   doesn't have enough money to pay for the groceries so
   she puts a few things back but when she goes to the
   clerk he tells her she still has to put more back. She does
   but decides she needs something so she brings it back.
   The clerk keeps complaining.
3. Two girls meet on a bus and talk about themselves and
   school.

A twelve-year-old from an underprivileged area submitted
these ideas. We had a lot of fun with the first especially:

1. The Mystery on Halloween Night

I think you should have a girl dressed up on Hallowe'en as a ghost, and as she goes trick or treating she meats with a real ghost, but she thinks it is just a person going trick or treating, but the ghost is really out for giving a trick.

2. Jeanny

I think you should have a girl, and her mother. The girl goes into her mother's bed room and use her make up mother comes in and scolds her for using her make up.

More Ideas for Two

1. A fan comes to get her favorite star's autograph. She knocks on the dressing-room door. She enters and finds the star drinking a glass of wine.
2. PLACE: School
   ACTORS: Principal, long-haired boy or miniskirted girl
   PLOT: The principal has called this boy or girl down to his office to do something about his long hair or her miniskirt.
3. a. A woman and a traveling salesman
   b. A stupid girl with a grocer
   c. A dressmaker with a girl who wants a wedding gown
   d. A girl and her mother when they find that their cat (which they thought was a Tom) has had kittens
   e. A woman trying to explain to her hairdresser how she wants her hair done
4. Two women are bragging about each other's husbands' jobs. One husband is a garbage man; the other is an architect.
5. Two actors are studying a script. They both want to be the star of the show.
6. A nurse is insisting that a patient take a bath. The patient doesn't want to.
7. PLACE: A carnival stand. The standkeeper keeps begging an old lady, who is winning everything, to go to another stand

because he's getting sold out. The old lady has very good luck at the stand, and she keeps getting all the prizes.

8. A girl thinks everyone hates her. She decides to be kind to those who are mean to her. She makes up with a girlfriend. Everything works out fine.

9. A pesky little brother keeps listening in to his older sister's phone conversations.

Things to Look For

In these early improvisations the teacher notices immediately everything the students lack. They have no idea where and how to stand so that they can be seen and heard. Sometimes they place important action in obscure areas, turning their backs on the audience. They don't know how to project their voices or assume importance. In the criticisms that follow each improvisation, the teacher and other students call attention to these faults. We try to correct them a little by discussing them. We urge the children to think of the action and where they will place their furniture so we can see and understand them better. As we progress in class, future lessons will solve many of these problems. Remember, we have only just begun.

Improvisations with two people have the following advantages:

1. They sharpen the child's awareness of the dramatic situation and how it is related to actual living experience. It gives him an opportunity to reenact his observations of life, which are acute in childhood. Remember, everything is still new to him. Life has not yet become boring.

2. They give him a better idea of plays and how they come to be.

3. They make him more conscious of the actor's responsibility to the play and the other actors.

An appointed stage manager always pulls the curtain for the performance of a playlet. He must listen for the curtain cue. This requires concentration. "Curtain!"

We Sigh with Success

As this lesson ends the teacher finds that she has experienced exhilaration when the children did something really good or when someone came exceptionally close to depicting real life! She can feel a sense of true satisfaction if she is sure that the children have grasped the idea of the unity an improvisation must have. Are they fairly well able to begin, give it some substance, and end it?

Before we say good-bye today, we inform everyone that next lesson we will be working on improvisations with one person.

Boys and girls, what do we mean when we do something *solo*? (*Answers here.*) That's right. Something alone. By ourselves. Well, that is what I want you to think about for next lesson— doing an improvisation alone. In this improvisation a person may be talking to himself or another person, but he is onstage alone. For instance, a lady is blind and alone. She awakes, goes through the everyday business of getting the paper at the front door, feeding her cat, getting herself something to eat. What would she say? Be sure to think of ideas that are confined to one place, like a room or a park bench. Don't spread your action too far. Are we certain now of what we are going to do? Bring in two good ideas for an improvisation with one person. See you soon.

Lesson 4

1. Today we work on improvisations with two people.
2. They require concentration, a word which we will discuss in class.
3. Make sure that you and your partner both understand your idea before you begin.
4. Speak clearly and distinctly.
5. Don't turn your back on the audience.
6. Keep your actions open to your audience. Let them see what you are doing. Remember, they must understand everything that is happening onstage.

7. Keep your idea on the trolley track.
8. When you are about to finish, bring your idea to an interesting end.

Assignment for next lesson:

At the next lesson we will do improvisations with *one* person. This will be our last assignment on improvisations for a while. Bring in two ideas for one person to work out.

LESSON 5

Improvisations with One Character

The improvisation with a single person is an opportunity for the child to release a great deal of the personal make-believe experience he has built up over the early childhood years. He is very experienced at this sort of thing, but how will he open up onstage? Sometimes we find he almost whispers. The prospect of playing alone before an audience is a little frightening for some. For others, it is precisely their cup of tea. They love it and are most at home here. In either case, the improvisation will play better if the teacher makes sure the child is working with a solid idea he knows how to carry through and bring to an end.

Boys and girls, do you remember at the last lesson I mentioned a word—solo—which means alone? Of course, you do. Solo comes from a Latin word, *solus*—alone. In long plays you sometimes find a character speaking a long speech by himself. This is called a *soliloquy*. It usually tells the audience a great deal of what this character is thinking. The Greeks, who were the first playwrights, called this a *monologue*. In Greek, *monos* means alone, or single —by himself. *Logos* means talk, or discourse. A monodrama is a drama acted or designed to be acted by one person. Drama also comes from a Greek word, meaning to act. Our improvisation today is based on these very old dramatic techniques. You are going to do an improvisation by yourself. In a sense it will be something like the make-believe play you amused yourself with when you didn't have a playmate not so long ago when you were smaller. Perhaps some of you even play like this occasionally now. But when we are onstage, we must attempt to dramatize our action for our audience. We must speak clearly, distinctly—loud enough for all to hear.

As we play out our idea we must keep our audience in mind. Are we interesting them, entertaining them? Are we following through with our idea? Are we making it go somewhere? Are we concentrating? Are we using our *imagination*? This is a very important word in acting—imagination. Who wants to tell me more about it? What is it, Phil? Yes, yes, a picture in our minds. That's right. Sally, what do you say? When you can taste something, and it isn't there. Good. Yes, we use our sense of taste to imagine a chocolate bar that isn't there, don't we? How about a pickle? Can you all taste a pickle right now? Well, you have told me, Phil, that to imagine something we must use our minds, isn't this right? Imagination helps us see something with our minds that really isn't present. It is a creation of our minds, a mental image. For some people, imagining is simple; for others it is difficult. Sometimes, in our imaginations, we see ourselves performing marvelous feats, don't we? Can you imagine a most beautiful rainbow, sparkling with colors of every hue, all of a sudden spring up before you? Have you got the image? (*Answers here.*) Now suppose you find that there are rungs in the rainbow like a ladder that you can climb. There you go—up, up—and over. You are scaling the rainbow, and soon you will be on the other side. What

A telephone is a universal 'prop' and very helpful in improvisations,
particularly with one person.

will you find there? I wonder. (*Many answers here.*) Yes, this is our imagination working for us, and it is a wonderful gift. Without it, how dull and uneventful life would be, wouldn't it? We would have no wonderful plays or stories or inventions. I hope it will help us to have good improvisations today. Let's get started, shall we?

One Alone

The teacher looks over today's ideas. Here are a few:

1. A person finds a wallet with money and a name and address in it. He's debating whether or not to return it to the owner. His conscience wins him over, so he returns the wallet, feeling very good.
2. A boy got a bad report card. He's thinking about how to tell his parents. He wants to beat around the bush, just slightly, so his parents won't get suspicious.
3. A person is locked in an old house on a stormy night and tries to get help.
4. A child gets up in the morning and gets ready for school.
5. One day a boy had just gotten a spanking. He was in his room talking very lowly about his mother.
6. A boy left in the morning without making his bed. His mother was very mad, and as she was making his bed she found a box of cookies.
7. A girl finds a big pumpkin in a pumpkin patch that she wants to make a jack-o-lantern of. But when she tries to pick it up it is too heavy to pick up.
8. A girl is in a store trying to pick out something for her mother's birthday. But she can't decide what to buy.
9. I think you should have a girl sitting in front of her mirror doing her hair and the mirror begins to talk. (Further probing revealed that the improvisation was to be based on the girl's reaction to the talking mirror.)

10. A new cheerleader for the Junior High School is to lead the cheers for the first time at tomorrow's game. She is afraid she will not remember her cheers and motions so she is practicing at home by herself.

11. A girl decides to try to bake a cake for the first time while her mother is away. She starts out O.K., but soon runs into trouble with measuring, mixing, pouring, and getting the pans into the hot oven. She ends up with a mountain of dirty dishes, and a cake that is a flop.

12. A person trying on shoes and never satisfied with a pair the lady brings her.

13. Going on a trip, packing a suitcase, going to the ticket office, and riding on a train. (This is a good idea in essence but is too involved. It covers too much territory. Packing a suitcase to go on a trip is enough to work with.)

14. A girl was combing her hair to go to a party. She was pulling and pulling and pulling the comb through her hair. Then she found out that someone had put gum on the comb and now the gum was in her hair.

15. A boy was sleeping and then the alarm clock rang and he gets up and sees that it's eight o'clock so he hurries up and gets dressed for school and then he looked at the calendar and it was Saturday so he went back to bed.

16. One afternoon after school a boy decided to go to his friend's house. He got home at seven and to his surprise found the door locked.

17. A girl is giving a lecture on self-discipline. At the climax of the lecture she forgets what to say. Her problem is to stall the audience without getting them bored.

18. A school teacher sends away for an item in the school newspaper. The teacher has lost the ten dollars that the students had given him to send away for the item.

He is at home thinking how to face them in the morning.
19. A person gets sick and nobody is home. What should that person do?
20. A girl has a book in her hand. She forgets she has the book in her hand and starts looking all over for it.
21. A woman is planning a trip to Europe.
22. A girl is trying to guess what she is getting for her birthday.
23. A park paper-picker walks along picking up papers with his pole and mumbling about the pay, saying he needs a raise to support his wife and kids.
24. PLACE: Home

    ACTOR: A little boy or girl

    PLOT: The boy or girl has broken something of value and is waiting for mother to come home to get the bad news.

Everyone of the above ideas has in it the germ for a dramatic monologue. Some offer a little more excitement than others. None are breathtakingly original. They are the norm. Yet, the experienced teacher knows that an extremely simple idea in the hands of a certain child can become a memorable improvisation. I am fairly certain that the above ideas belong to the children. They have thought of them themselves. After absorbing them, we find them to have the essence of childhood experience or reflect a child's reaction to an incident.

Developing Discipline

If there is time, it is interesting to let several children work with the same idea. Encourage simplicity of detail. Restrict it to a simple setting. No matter how imaginative and talented the youngster may be, he needs strong guidance in this area. Motivate him to begin it, give it some substance, (that is, reveal the idea to us), and bring it to an interesting end. This type of discipline, early in the course, is very helpful to the child in other ways. It helps him develop judgment and se-lectivity. The moderate criticisms that follow each improvisa-tion also help him to learn what is essential and interesting, what is unnecessary and dull.

Improvisations, at this point, have gently opened the chil-dren's inexperienced eyes to the stage and what we do on it and with it. They subtly instruct them in what the stage is for.

I think it is very important that the children learn from the start that people come to the theater to be entertained, amused, excited, that the audience who comes to watch expects some-thing from the actors. This engenders a respect for the art. By stressing the importance of concentration, imagination, the health and grace of the body, and the development of a good voice and distinctive speech, the teacher engenders respect for the time-honored art of acting.

Children, we are going to spend the next few lessons paying close attention to our speech. We know that the actor's most im-portant tool is his body. Every part of it must function well, especially the vocal organs, since an actor would be quite useless without his voice. From when you leave class until your next lesson I want you to pay particularly close attention to the speech of those around you. Jot down on a piece of paper a list of ten speech faults you have observed while listening to those around you. These must be faults directly related to speech, not to how we stand or what we do when we talk, but how we speak, what mistakes we make. We will discuss your lists at the next lesson. Good-bye till then.

Lesson 5

1. Today we do improvisations alone.
2. When a character talks alone onstage in a play, this is called a soliloquy. This word has in it the Latin word *solus*, which means alone.
3. When one person works on a long speech or conversation, we

also call this a monologue. This word comes from two Greek words, *monos* and *logos*, meaning to speak alone.

4. Working alone is not entirely new to you, because you have probably played make-believe alone many times when you were smaller.

5. When we make believe alone we play by ourselves or invent another person to talk with.

6. That is precisely what you will be doing in your improvisation today.

7. Doing improvisations alone forces you to use CONCENTRATION and IMAGINATION.

8. What is imagination?

9. Enjoy your improvisations today. Earnestly concentrate on entertaining your audience.

10. Begin to think about your audience and how the actor is related to it.

Assignment for next lesson:

We are going to start to think about our speech—how we talk. I want you to observe the speech of those around you. List ten speech faults that you have observed in others. We will discuss them next week.

Attending to Our Speech

LESSON 6

Articulation and Expression

The question arises: How do we handle speech in a class of this type? Since drama is our primary concern, how much emphasis do we place upon speech, certainly an important acting tool? Remember that the children are having their initial experience with drama. It is my feeling that too much preoccupation with speech at this level often discourages and dampens the spirit. Speech should be introduced briefly, for the sole purpose of convincing the child that work in dramatics requires careful speech and that successful actors have spent years studying speech to perfect their voices. "This is something that *we* are just beginning to do," the teacher reminds the class, not expecting perfection. Of course, there are children who even at this age easily grasp the fundamentals of speech. But we are enjoying drama now, not speech, and should keep this in mind.

Let's Articulate

The assignment given at the last lesson asked each child to bring in a list of ten speech faults, or bad speech habits, he has observed in others. Before collecting these today, the teacher asks him to discuss one fault on his list. We do this hoping he will begin to listen critically to the speech of those around him, to differentiate between careful and sloppy speech, and to articulate properly himself. Then the teacher begins to explain articulation.

> Boys and girls, we all know that these bodies of ours are wonderful things, quite capable of performing marvelous feats— thinking, walking, feeling, smelling, seeing, hearing, and talking, of course. Most of us are generously gifted with a good mind, a healthy body, hands, feet, ears, nose, eyes, and a mouth. Every part of us is vitally important to our physical well-being, and if we were deprived of any one of them, we would certainly feel a great loss. But let's concentrate for a moment, shall we, on our mouths. First of all, what do we have mouths for? (*Many answers here.*) What do we find in our mouths? (*More hands.*) That's right, Cindy. A tongue! And Ronald says lips. Good for you, Arlene—our gums! Haven't we forgotten something? A very important item! Right, Jack! Our teeth! Remember, it was Little Red Riding Hood who said, "Oh, Grandma, what big teeth you have!" And when the wolf replied, "The better to eat you with, my dear!" he wasn't just kidding, we know, for our teeth are invaluable and certainly aid us in the eating and digestive processes. They are also very necessary for clear, understandable speech. Let's all be quiet for a moment and think of anyone we know who does not have teeth. How does he look without them? How does he talk? What sounds are difficult for him to make?

Now we are in for a discussion of relatives with false teeth, but this is good because it introduces the topic of articulation. Since the mouth, with its makeup of teeth, lips, tongue, gums, and soft and hard palate, is the chief organ of articulation, and children are familiar with their own mouths, this is a simple way to begin. I briefly stress the importance of all parts of the mouth in the overall function of speech, explaining that we need jaws to form sounds and a nimble tongue tip to form clean-cut consonants.

After the teacher has given an explanation of articulation, she may have the children recite simple, routine word exercises to make sure that they are aware of how to use the different articulators.

1. Lips and tongue help to differentiate between these words:

     VILE—VOWEL
     TRIAL—TROWEL
     TILE—TOWEL
     FILE—FOWL

2. We need our lips to make firm *m* and *b* sounds:

     HUM   HUMMING
     COME   COMING
     SOME   SUMMER
     DIM   DIMMER
     RUB   RUBBER
     BUG   BUGGY
     RIB   RIBBON
     FIB   FIBBING
     DON'T MOLLYCODDLE MOLLY, MOM,
     WHILE MIMI'S IN MIAMI.

3. Lips round and stretch as they form:

     EE—OO—EE—OO—EE—OO
     AY—OH—AY—OH—AY—OH

4. The tongue and the teeth help us to say these words:
   a. TED TOLD A TALE TITLED TOM TIT TOT.
   b. Distinguish between *ts* and *dz* sounds in word endings:

     BEATS   BEADS
     BITS   BIDS
     CENTS   SENDS

CARTS   CARDS
WATTS   WADS
PATS   PADS

c. Distinguish between *d* and *t* sounds.

KIDDY   KITTY
MEDAL   METAL
PEDAL   PETAL
BIRD   BERT
MADDER   MATTER
FEED   FEET
BED   BET
NEED   NEAT
DEAD   DEBT
WADING   WAITING

Painting Your Words

Children respond instinctively to the beauty of words, and when a word or combination of words is aesthetically appealing, they really try to say them with care and feeling. Here is a list the teacher may have them read individually, encouraging them to enunciate with feeling and sound syllables and word endings carefully:

KING TUT'S TOMB
THE ICE PALACE
A CHEST OF JEWELS
CRYSTAL LIGHT
THE WIZARD OF OZ
MUDDY MUD PIES
A TINKLING SOUND
CREAMY CARAMELS
THE PRINCESS AND THE PEA
QUEEN CELESTE

MERLIN THE MIGHTY MAGICIAN
BOOMLAY, BOOMLAY, BOOMLAY, BOOM
BLACK AS A WITCH'S CAT
A TERRIFYING TIGER
GOLD, FRANKINCENSE, AND MYRRH
THE MISTY SEA
A WOODEN SHOE
HUSH, HUSH, HUSH
THINKING THOUGHTS OF THISTLES
THE FAIRY THEA
DAINTY, DELICATE CHINA
THE IVORY DOOR

Children, as you read these words, I want you to imagine that your mouths are magic, capable of manufacturing silver sounds, golden tones, precious stones, whatever you like. I want you to feel that your words are both precious and powerful and that only you have the ability to make them as careful and colorful as the plumage on a peacock. Try to feel that you can paint them as you say them.

If there is time and the teacher wishes, she may ask each child to choose one of the above phrases and work it into a clear, articulate, imaginative sentence to be uttered by a character whom he creates himself. He is to enter the stage alone and say this sentence very carefully, but *in* character. If he feels his character needs some explanation, he should do so before he starts the sentence. He may accompany this with some stage business if he likes, but the idea is to keep this assignment simple and restricted to the single element of careful and expressive speech.

Lesson 6 ends with the teacher urging the children to review what they have done in class several times throughout the next week: "Remember to look at your lesson sheet daily and work on all the articulation words that require care and attention."

Lesson 6

1. The first thing we do today is have each student tell us about one speech fault that he has observed in others during the past week.
2. After your teacher collects your lists and discusses the qualities of good and poor speakers, she will begin to explain to you the process of ARTICULATION.
3. Articulation is the utterance of clear and distinct syllables. It means you must pronounce your words with care and precision. Do not overarticulate, or you will sound unnatural.
4. You articulate correctly when you pronounce these words carefully:

picnic	new	pitcher
pumpkin	aluminum	just
poem	library	for
chimney	children	get
February	interesting	poetry
really	education	athletic
film	surprise	cinnamon
dial	picture	didn't

5. Words with *d, t, l,* and *th* require a tongue that is not lazy:

better	butter	metal	pretty
bright	light	mitten	kept
ladder	mad	pedal	daffodil
iodine	dead	ditty	paddle
lily	William	veil	Alice
little	yellow	apple	Emily Lee
depth	thin	the	thread
fifth	thick	then	feather

Assignment for next lesson:

Please review carefully all that you accomplished during your lesson today. Go over the words above carefully and often before we meet again. Next week we begin work on a very short playlet requiring good articulation. Remember, an actor must have especially careful speech—so practice often.

LESSON 7

Articulation and Pronunciation

Today's lesson is a continuation of Lesson 6, emphasizing the care we should take in pronouncing words. The teacher explains to the children that there are standards of good speech; that people around them may not be speaking with careful pronunciation, but this does not mean that they should not attempt to do so.

We begin this lesson by reviewing the material distributed last week. If time permits, each child should have the experience of reciting aloud as many of these exercises as possible. The teacher may also want to finish or review the sentence assignment we began toward the end of the lesson. In order to make sure the children understand that some speech faults are the result of a physical problem, the teacher goes into a short explanation of a sound like *s*.

I'm sure, boys and girls, that many of you know other children who *lisp*. Lisping shows up in a person's speech predominantly when he cannot make a good *s* sound. For instance, he says yeth for yes. It is also noticeable in other sounds, but we will consider *s* today. Lisping occurs when a boy or girl either *cannot* or *doesn't know how* to use his tongue correctly. Sometimes his tongue is too long, and sometimes it is just plain lazy. Remember, the tongue is a muscle that needs proper exercise, too. In either case, he must try to use his tongue correctly. Then, too, the *s* sound doesn't sound quite right if a child has spaces between his teeth or if he uses too much breath. Remember that *s* is the snake sound and must have a hiss to it, but not enough to make it unpleasant. Let's hear how you sound when you say *s*.

1. Here are some words that have *s* at their beginning, middle, or end:

STONE	FUSSING	HOUSE
STORY	MUSTARD	MOSS
SUE	BISCUIT	ACE
SOUP	MASTER	MISS
SUN	BOSSY	PURSE
SAP	BASKET	ICE

2. These words end with *s*, *se*, and *z* but all get a *z* pronounciation:

APPEASE	BOYS	DOORS	CARS
AMUSE	FIZZ	FURS	DOES
BURNS	WHOSE	AS	RISE

The second half of the lesson today is devoted to work on a very short scene which incorporates the following list of words. These are words which obviously get mispronounced, mostly through carelessness. First, the teacher has the students run through the word list, and they discuss its treatment.

just	government	won't you	horrible
picture	would you	for	horrid
pitcher	could you	get	Washington
picnic	didn't you	forehead	wash
Harry	foreign	new	Dorothy
hairy	forest	knew	half—have

After she feels the class understands how the words should be pronounced, the teacher asks two children to read the scene.

Phoning requires careful speech at all times and so does acting! Both characters in this scene must articulate distinctly.

The two characters are Mother and Pat. The part of Pat is interchangeable and can be played by either a boy or a girl. If there is time, all members of the class should read at least one of the parts today. Sometimes, in a small class, we play the scene often enough so that one person can play both roles. If this is the case, so much the better. The staging is simple. Be sure to have both characters facing the audience. Here is a suggested ground plan:

(*The scene is a living room. The mother is at the desk writing.*)

PAT: (*Enters hurriedly looking for something.*) Gosh, I'm late!

MOTHER: Won't you please tell me why you're in such a hurry?

PAT: I have to be there early with half of the class.

MOTHER: You look horrible in that horrid sweater, and you have a smudge on your forehead.

PAT: Just for once can't I leave early? I have to meet Harry.

MOTHER: How are you getting there?

PAT: Dorothy's mother is taking us, and I have to be there at half past ten.

MOTHER: The picnic will wait, and so will Dorothy and Harry. Are they going to take pictures?

PAT: Yes, and I have to bring a pitcher for the lemonade.

MOTHER: Tell Harry I hope he doesn't get a spider bite this time.

PAT: Gosh, yes! Remember, I told him, "There's a spider. That spider's hairy, Harry!" But he didn't hear me. By the way, Harry's friend is coming from Forest Lane, Washington.

MOTHER: Is that the boy whose father is a foreign correspondent for the government?

PAT: Yes, he was here last summer.

MOTHER: Well, have fun. Wear your new sweater; wash your face; and don't keep them waiting.

Before this lesson ends the teacher should cast this scene and, if possible, block it. She should make sure that each child knows his part and that he must learn his lines *word perfect* for the next lesson. This is important, because at this stage of learning, sometimes children are apt to substitute other words for these fairly simple ones.

Boys and girls, as you learn your lines for our little scene during the coming week, I want you to make a special effort to memorize each word exactly as the author intended. In this case the author is a playwright. That is the name we give a person who writes dialogue, or a play script. Although, this is very short, it is nevertheless dialogue, and you must learn it exactly as it was written. The words are simple but important to our lesson and our work. Good-bye now. See you next week.

Lesson 7

1. Today we begin class by reviewing exercises from last week.
2. We are still concerned with articulation, pronouncing all word syllables carefully.
3. A frequent mistake in articulation is not pronouncing the *ing* in words with this ending. Take time with it.
     What are you doing?
     I'm coming.
     swimming and boating
     coming and going
4. These words require smooth enunciation:

didn't you	can't you	don't you
wouldn't you	have you	won't you
couldn't you	I have to	we should have

5. Work on these words carefully for your scene next lesson:

just	government	won't you	horrible
picture	would you	for	horrid
pitcher	could you	get	Washington
picnic	didn't you	forehead	wash
Harry	foreign	new	Dorothy
hairy	forest	knew	half—have

6. After you have read your scene, discussed the words, and the parts are given out, start thinking about how you are going to play your role next week.

7. Remember, both parts require careful, articulate speech.

Assignment for next lesson:

Think often during the coming week of the work we did in class today. Practice all the words on this lesson sheet. Learn your part carefully. Next week we will do this scene without our scripts.

LESSON 8

Articulation and the Script

Although some of the children in class may have been in school plays, this is our first experience with a memorized script in drama class. Of course, it is a very short scene. We are concentrating on good, careful speech in this lesson. Nevertheless, the teacher should expect the children to be so caught up with the enthusiasm of acting (many of them for the first time) that they will forget their careful speech and tend to change the dialogue and substitute words of their own, which changes the whole idea of the lesson. We should be prepared for this, and this is why we wish to keep the scene simple.

Getting Down to Business

It is well to give both characters a small amount of *business* —that is, action or gesture—in this scene, but nothing so intricate that they become too involved in it. After Pat enters, he may appear to be searching for a picnic item he left there earlier in the morning—the pitcher perhaps. Mother may rise and put a book from her desk into the bookcase before she crosses to him and examines his face and the smudge. This is entirely up to the teacher, but she should remember that whatever she asks the child to do in this simple scene should not distract him from the purpose of our lesson—good articulation. If this assignment seems a breeze for a confident, articulate child, he can coordinate extra movement. If another child has difficulty with the lines, I would suggest no business at all for him. It is not really necessary. The class may play the scene as often as the teacher likes until she feels they have really grasped the idea of the lesson. Parts may be exchanged, and if she desires, the teacher may have the class repeat the scene, with the reassigned parts, at next week's lesson.

Back to Good Speech

The second half of Lesson 8 we spend distributing and explaining another assignment on articulation, which the children are to learn during the coming week and present next lesson in class, when we finalize our unit on speech. This is an exercise in imagination and pantomime as well. The teacher gives each child the following five verses with the lesson sheet:

1. I'm Kookie, the coy Kangaroo.
   EE—OO—EE—OO—EE—OO
   Hippety hop and away I go.
   A—OH—A—OH—A—OH
2. I'm prickly Pete Prangle the Bear,
   With a jar of prick prangly pears,
   Which I'll put on a shelf
   To eat all by myself
   In my lily bell cell of a lair.
3. My name is Byron the Bee.
   Ho hum diddle hum diddle hee

    I like to go buzzin'
    And visit my cousin,
    Sweet little Emily Lee.

4. I'm Willie the Wolf.
    Hear me snarl.
    I slither, I slink, and I crawl.
    Some call me William. Some call me Bill.
    Dance Willie, prance Willie, silly old Will.

5. I'm Piper the Pig.
    I'm a pearl
    A jewel, a whirl of a pearl.
    I like pickled peppers, the pecks that I've picked.
    I lick, and I pick, and I never get sick.

The teacher asks each child to learn each of the five verses, paying particular attention to word pronunciation and word endings. The verses are musical and easy to learn. He is also to prepare a pantomime, simple and short, that suits each animal and the bee. This pantomime is done after he has said the verse. We hope the child will begin to feel free with his voice as he says these verses, at the same time assuming a slight burden of articulation and characterization. For this is basically what the actor is required to do when he acts—incorporate the physical and imaginative with good speech.

We end class today reminding everyone that next week we will do our verses and pantomimes for the whole class. "Let's see how much like the animals and the bee we can make our bodies behave." The children will also have an opportunity to play another role in the scene with Mother and Pat. "What a busy lesson we are going to have! Please, don't forget to bring your best speech with you."

Lesson 8

1. Today we are going to act.
2. Our scene is both an acting and a speech exercise.

3. There are two characters: Mother and Pat.
4. Both of them articulate very carefully all the while they discuss the picnic.
5. After everyone in class has had a chance to play the scene at least once, your teacher is going to give you a copy of five short speech-pantomime exercises.
6. She will read these with you in class. They, too, require careful articulation.
7. As you read each verse be sure to give careful attention to all syllables, especially word endings. Pay close attention to *l* in Verse 4. It needs a nimble tongue.

Assignment for next lesson:

Learn each of the verses we read today in class: the Kangaroo, the Bear, the Bee, the Wolf, the Pig. Prepare a short pantomime that each would do after you have said the verse. The verses are simple but require careful articulation. Learn them very carefully. Be absolutely certain of your pantomimes. We will do them at the next lesson.

LESSON 9

Articulation and Movement

With this lesson we finish our unit on speech. Depending upon the time limit and the number of children in class, the teacher may review a little bit of everything from the preceding lessons, or she may spend a short time reviewing the scene with

Mother and Pat, or she may devote the entire time to the speech pantomime exercise we are going to do today.

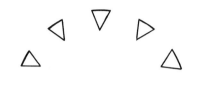

Our Voice in Verse

We begin by asking five children to come to Center Stage. They arrange themselves in a semicircle, as above. Each child says the verse, then moves into the center area for the pantomime, and when he has finished, retreats into place again. After all five have said one verse and performed a pantomime, they exchange places and repeat until each has said all five verses. Then they are replaced by a new group. We repeat until the class has completed the exercise. These verses are simple and should provoke the children into a characteristic pantomime. The pantomime gives them freedom, as well as energy and enthusiasm for the next verse. The teacher encourages the children to relax as they speak and move:

> Try to make your movements big and easy so that we can easily see and understand what you want us to see. Remember, these characters are very articulate. Think of very articulate cartoon characters who speak with great care and precision. They may certainly be funny if you wish them to be.

Overcarefulness of speech is to some degree what we want in this exercise. If the children assume too much affectation, the teacher should correct them, of course. Animal characters give them a chance to indulge in some sort of vocal characterization, so we must expect this. Handling better speech while assuming character and movement is a big job for beginners. If at the end of this exercise the teacher feels that the class is looser of tongue and freer of body, she can consider the exercise successful.

The Sound of Music

Since the next unit is devoted to musical pantomime, which must be explained carefully at the next lesson when there is more time, the teacher leaves the students today asking them to take a close look at the record collection at home if there is one. She wants them to think about the records they are familiar with, the types, the various speeds. She asks them to listen to records during the time until the next lesson. It doesn't matter whether they are old or new records.

Try to listen to a number of musical records, children. We are not interested in records with voices singing. We simply want to hear music. While we listen to each record, let's try to decide how we could tell a good story in movement to it. What kind of a pantomime does this record inspire? Do a lot of listening. If you do not have a phonograph, perhaps you may listen to that of a relative or friend. Try to decide the type of record you like best. Remember, listen carefully.

Lesson 9

1. This is our last lesson on the unit of speech and articulation.
2. Today we will quickly review the work of the past three lessons.
3. If there is time, your teacher will repeat the Mother and Pat scene.
4. Try to imagine that you have a very enthusiastic audience for your speech-pantomime verses.
5. Enunciate clearly, and relax for your pantomime.
6. Try to bring a different quality to each character.
7. An actor cannot be good without good speech and clean-cut movement.
8. Most of all, have fun doing these exercises.

Assignment for next lesson:

Listen to as many musical records as you can in the intervening time until our next lesson. They should be musical records without a vocal accompaniment. As you listen, try to imagine dramatic situations that might be performed with the music. Supply as many ideas as possible to the records you particularly like.

PART IV

Miming and Music

Explaining the Assignment

Children respond intuitively and intensely to music. This response not only indicates the degree of feeling the child has for rhythm, but reveals a number of other aptitudes as well. Therefore, we include the simple exercise of the record pantomime in the first-year curriculum.

We invite our first audience to the demonstration of this pantomime. Why? Because the children are ready for an audience, and this is the type of performance that will guarantee the reasonable amount of success necessary to encourage beginners. We must remember that many of the children have never performed before. Placing them in a play right off the bat imposes a lot of needless worries that they shouldn't be at all concerned with. The responsibility of lines, movement, and business, coupled with inexperience, usually makes their first experience with an audience frightening and substandard. We feel that a musical pantomime, which is concerned mainly with free movement, is a better choice for our first presentation.

Practicing Our Pantomimes

This record pantomime is simply a prepared pantomime done to the background of a musical recording. The child may choose any type of record that appeals to him, without a vocal accompaniment, of course. The first two lessons in class will reveal whether or not the choice of record is workable. After he has chosen a record to his liking, the child listens to it several times, picturing an incident in action that will be suitable to the mood and rhythm of the music. His choice of music and action definite, he begins to rehearse and work out his story pantomimically, setting his own stage, inventing his own action. The children present these pantomimes several times, throughout seven lessons, adding and subtracting ideas with the help of criticisms from the class.

We spend seven lessons on this exercise because it has various merits:

1. It is a fun exercise and relaxes the child.
2. We learn the kind of imagination he has and how he uses it.
3. We discover to what degree he has:
   a. a sense of rhythm
   b. a sense of timing
   c. a sense of body control.
4. We learn how well the child can sustain the mood of the music in the movements he creates. Can he sustain this mood?
5. The child learns the responsibility of working alone, creating something himself.
6. Each child learns much about his fellow classmates. He is impressed by the carefulness and originality of others where it exists.

Choose a Familiar Idea

When the teacher introduces this exercise to the class, she should prepare a pantomime herself, bring the record to class, and demonstrate it. This is the best way to make certain the children understand what they must do. For this demonstration I usually choose gay, lighthearted music—a waltz or a polka or such a classic as Dave Rose's "Holiday for Strings." It is best to choose an action that is familiar to the children. Such a simple idea as getting up late and rushing to school or work appeals to them. I rush into the bathroom, wash, brush my teeth, rush to get dressed, rush to eat, rush, rush, rush to get the bus—and as the music tapers off to a finale I invent a suitable ending to accompany it.

Making It Clear

During this lesson the teacher should take a great deal of time to explain all the details. She must make certain of the type of phonograph she will have at her disposal. How many speeds will it play? She should find out which child does not have a phonograph in his home. Then she will have to suggest how he may rehearse his record pantomime. Perhaps a relative or friend has a phonograph.

The teacher should discourage any child's choice of a long symphonic record that will have to be spotted. Sometimes this is the only record the child can find at home, and the teacher may never learn that he is not permitted to buy a new one. Occasionally we encounter this. It is rare, but it does happen. It is all the more puzzling when parents pay to enroll their child in a course, evidently thinking it worthwhile to let him pursue this interest. Their lack of cooperation is embarrassing and frustrating for the child, and the teacher can choose to handle it either by phoning the parents and explaining the necessity of the record or simply by having several tried and true records of her own on hand. The latter solution is sometimes the best, because it solves the problem sooner, and the teacher knows that the child will have something to get started with immediately, without his having to wait until the record is purchased.

It is also best to choose a record that is single or segmented, one that begins and ends within a 2½ to 3 minute section. The teacher should stress several times that the record must have no vocal accompaniment—in fact, no voice of any kind at all. There is really no hard-and-fast rule about what kind of record we should choose. Classical or modern, it makes no difference, as long as it appeals to the imagination of the child and is an inspiration to him. Children often surprise us with an outdated selection from the past. Only how the music strikes their fancy is important.

After the teacher feels that her demonstration pantomime is satisfactory, she gives the children their assignment for the next lesson:

> Boys and girls, I want you to select a record, as I have done today. I want you to select an idea for a pantomime to go with it, and I want you to bring it to class next lesson. As I mentioned before, be sure your record does not have singing or talking of any kind. In order to choose a record you like, you may have to listen to several of them. As you listen to them, try to picture in your mind a story idea. After you have made your choice, play your record several times and begin to build your pantomime story to fit the music. We are going to spend several lessons working on this pantomime. At the last lesson we will present it to your parents and friends. Be sure to pick a record you really like, because you will be working with it quite awhile. Are there any questions?

Lesson 10

1. Today we start work on a new assignment.
2. This is an exercise which helps the beginning actor develop a sense of rhythm and body control.
3. It is also an exercise in movement. In it we move to music.
4. If you have studied music, you already know that rhythm is very important to a good musician and a good dancer.
5. An actor must also have a sense of rhythm for speaking and moving.
6. This record will have no singing or vocalization of any sort. The

actor must invent an idea or story in movement which will correspond to the rhythm and mood of the music.

7. If the music is slow, you certainly wouldn't work out an idea around a man rushing to work in the morning. If the music is fast, your idea wouldn't center around a man who is fishing lazily on a summer day.

8. As your teacher plays this record think of ideas to improvise which you feel will go with the music.

Assignment for next lesson:

Bring a record to class next week—one without vocal accompaniment, just music. You are going to perform a record pantomime at the end of the semester. Here are some ideas on how to select your record:

a. Sit and listen to a number of records you like.

b. As you listen to them try to think of a story idea.

c. Play the record that seems to present the best idea for a story, and try to build your pantomime to suit the music.

LESSON 11

Discussing Each Selection

The children wear a different expression today as they settle down in their seats! They have been listening! If they have listened correctly, they have been listening imaginatively, creatively. Some have confidently worked out an idea that they feel will be met with approval. Others bring a record but have no idea what they will do. They need help. There may be some who have yet to select a record. They may have received no help from home.

Discuss Each Selection

Usually the teacher will meet with a variety of problems at the onset of this exercise. Hopefully she will be able to settle most of them during this lesson. She must be prepared for a few surprises concerning record selections. Most of the children, because they have phonographs and record collections at home, will have no trouble selecting a record. This does not always mean it will be a good choice. Old records are sometimes difficult to play with new needles. If a child has no record and phonograph at home, with no place to rehearse a pantomime, as I stated in the previous chapter, it is a good idea for the teacher to have a few time-tested records of her own on hand.

As we play each record today, watch what the children have prepared, and listen to their ideas of what they want to do with their records, we make sure that they understand the basic requirements for a good record pantomime:

1. The idea should have a good incident behind it, in which something happens.
2. We should not plan just one action for the whole record. That would be very boring.
3. The music imposes a mood—light or happy, sad or serious —which we are called upon to obey.
4. Your body is most important in this exercise, and you must work to make it respond to the mood of the music.
5. Since we are going to invite your parents and relatives to watch you present these pantomimes, you must select an idea that you know is going to appeal to an audience— an idea that has an action that they will enjoy watching.

Pantomimes on Parade

Now, let us take a look at one of the ideas. First we shall play John's record.

What have you selected, John? Let me see? This is a long-playing record, speed 33, entitled *The American Composers Hall of Fame*. The first segment is an American classic, "Lazybones," which has been very popular here in America for many years. It was written by a famous composer of our time, Hoagy Carmichael. Suppose you tell us your idea, John.

John, who is eleven, tells us that he is going to carry out the theme the title suggests—he is going to be a lazy man getting up in the morning. He goes through the ordinary routine of arising, washing, shaving, eating breakfast. But it is a struggle, because he is tired and can't seem to really awaken. As he starts to leave for work he realizes it is raining. He gets an umbrella, starts out to work. On the way fatigue takes over again, and he sits on a park bench to rest. He starts to nod and falls asleep sitting up. He awakens again, sharply, and looks at his watch but can't get started. So sleep finally overcomes him again. He lies down on the bench. The umbrella falls to the ground, and as the record drifts off to an ending, John drifts off to sleep.

We have to agree as we watch that this pantomime needs work. The business of washing, shaving, and eating needs much more pantomimic care. But the idea is basically sound and shows the imagination and thought that went into it. John is on the right track. He should keep his idea but work hard on it.

Remember, John, such a little thing as looking in the mirror requires you to look straight ahead, as you would in your own mirror. Keep your eyes up, straight ahead. Then our audience will feel that they are watching a true incident, something that is really happening.

Wanda has chosen a sprightly modern piece, "Just Imagine," by DeSylva, Brown, and Henderson. She envisions an old lady with a cane walking in the park who comes upon a young couple, obviously in love, seated upon a park bench. The happiness of the young couple, along with the feeling of spring in the air, rejuvenates the old lady. She feels gay and young again. While eavesdropping she drops her cane and begins to dance a little before leaving the happy scene as the music fades.

As Wanda goes through this for the first time we observe that she is putting more effort into her dancing than into the character of the old lady. We point out that we get absolutely no feeling of age. This is something she must develop as rehearsals continue. Also she must set her stage more definitely. Where is the bench going to be? Where is she going to drop her cane? This business must be definite and remain the same throughout the rehearsals.

Colleen, who has a good sense of character, has chosen a well-known selection, Xavier Cugat's "Tico Tico." She is going to be a busy waitress in a hash joint who is the only one on duty during the rush hour. Although her character, walk, and manner seem pretty well thought out, we suggest that during future rehearsals she must plan her action so that we see more of the front of her than the back of her.

Since, at this stage of their training, the children know very little of stage mechanics, we can expect many mistakes in this area. The teacher should not discourage the children with too much criticism in this direction. She cannot expect to iron out every technical flaw. What we are after is the essence of their ideas and how well they are able to capture them in movement.

Of course, every idea is not suited to the mood or theme of the chosen record for various reasons. Sometimes we find that the child doesn't really have a complete idea in his mind or that what he has worked out is either too fast or too slow and monotonous for the demands of the tempo and very inhibiting.

Occasionally we find that a child has worked out a pantomime that is quite detailed and studied but in rather poor taste for his age and for presentation with the rest of the group. Such an example is Cheryl's idea. She is an exceptionally pretty and rather precocious youngster of eleven, who, with parental suggestion, decided to portray a serious study of an alcoholic man. She is a little chagrined when we urge her to abandon this idea for another, but there is really little sense in continuing with it. If she were sixteen or seventeen, we would reconsider, but several factors compel this decision. First of all, she is only eleven and we don't think it fair that she should preoccupy herself with this idea over an extended period of time. It also has a tendency to stimulate the others to choose topics that they are curious about but unfamiliar with. We do not want to cause unnecessary criticism or embarrassment for the child when the day of presentation arrives.

As it turned out, Cheryl arrived at the next lesson with a completely prepared pantomime, in which she was a bank robber. Sharon chose to be a desperado to the background of Gounod's "Funeral March." Very often, girls of this age are as much preoccupied with ideas of adventure and excitement as the boys, and it is well to let them experiment with them. As a general rule, I do not encourage the girls to play boys and vice versa, but there are times when a child seems really stumped for an idea or determined to get one out of his system, so I permit it.

Kevin is going to do a tipsy waiter to the background of "The Blue Danube Waltz," and this is all right, because he is working it out with a light touch that is charming and amusing, if a little uncontrolled.

Before this lesson ends, the teacher should make sure that each student departs with a workable theme which he can rehearse at home. If it is absolutely impossible for a child to come up with an idea of his own, whether he has a record or not, the teacher should supply him with one that she feels he is capable of carrying out.

Remember, children, to listen to your record often. As you listen to your record, jot down your ideas on paper as they come to you. Work your incident into a little story. It must begin and end in an interesting fashion. Your body is important. Try to make your body obey the tempo of the music, but don't think of yourself as a dancer. From now until I see you again spend most of your time making your idea complete so that you can rehearse with a feeling of confidence, knowing exactly what you are going to do. Then we can spend our time in class making your record interesting and exciting. Until I see you again—have fun!

Lesson 11

1. Today we will play the record you have brought to class, and your teacher and classmates will make suggestions for the pantomime idea that you have created to go with the music.

2. At first you may have many ideas. From all of these you must select the one that you think best suits the music.

3. Of course, you must pick an idea that you know is going to appeal to the audience. This is the musical pantomime that you will give for your parents and friends at the end of the semester.

4. Your idea should have a good story behind it, in which something happens—an incident. You should not plan just one action for the whole record. This would be very boring.

5. Your record may be old or new. It makes no difference, as long as you can tell us a good story with movement to music.

6. Body coordination is very important to the actor, and this group of lessons is designed to give you good body coordination through the use of music. Every actor must know how to respond correctly to the mood of a play. We need rhythm to interpret mood.

7. This is one of two very important projects for beginners. You will spend several lessons working on this exercise. Since there is a performance involved, we expect you to do the very best you can do with this assignment.

8. Ideas and rehearsal on your musical improvisation should not

stop today after your drama class is over and start again at the next lesson. Keep working on it a little every day.

Assignment for next lesson:

Now that your teacher has approved your idea, start to rehearse your musical record improvisation. Be sure to work it out carefully so that everyone who watches it believes it. Have it ready for the next lesson.

LESSON 12

Completing Our Ideas

We spend today helping the child complete his story idea, work it out in sequence, and answer any question he may have concerning it. We call upon each child individually and play his record to see what he has accomplished on his own.

Be Simple and Selective

We urge him to listen to the rhythm of the music and respond accordingly with simple body responses. His body is telling what happens. In this exercise the child is at first inclined to use his feet alone as he strives to obey the various rhythms that the music dictates. But if the character he has chosen to portray is a strong individual type placed in an interesting setting, various, well-chosen bits of business will enable him to use his face, arms, and hands with an ease that grows out of the character. The business should be selective and kept at a minimum. The child should not be burdened with too many details.

Margie, a nine-year-old, has decided to be a very fussy lady who enters an expensive restaurant, sits, and ponders over the menu. She is very demanding, and the imaginary waiter is kept very busy giving her every attention. As she is about to pay the bill we discover she has forgotten her money, and she ends her pantomime having to wash the dishes. Since the movement in this idea is simple (she sits through most of it), we encourage her to use her face, hands, and body to express her character. Her walk, as she enters to the slow, bluesy beat of "Blues in the Night," is pompous and overbearing. We see disgust and frustration written all over her as she rolls up her sleeves to wash the dishes at the sink we have placed Down Left to make sure the audience will see the ending.

The teacher will find that she will have to give much help and suggestion in planning where the action will take place so that everything the children do onstage will be clearly visible to onlookers. She must not be disappointed with careless pantomimic detail or poor coordination. An excellence in these qualities in a child so young is usually an indication of very promising dramatic ability, but shy, inexperienced youngsters sometimes acquire this in time. Pantomime is a great art that has never been widely developed or used in this country, where only a handful of performers, mostly comedians, use it. It takes talent, time, skill, and care to develop it. Drama schools use it as part of their training, but, on the whole, I feel that they do not use it enough. This kind of exercise reveals very quickly to the experienced teacher the depth of sensitivity possessed by each individual in the class. If we know this, we know a great deal about each child.

Don't Forget Your Character

We are insistent when we demand to know, "What type of person are you? Do you walk as your character would walk? Do you react to things as he would? What are his mannerisms?"

If the child has decided to put an imaginary character in the pantomime with him, he must realize that he has to work hard to convince us that he is present.

We find, too, that if we can get the boy or girl to immerse himself in the character's funniness or sadness or madness or gladness, he will relax more easily, and other nuances of the character's movements will come naturally.

If the class is large, the teacher will have to curtail her remarks. Suggestions and changes will have to be very pertinent and selective. Be sure you do not confuse the child with too many changes or discourage him with too many criticisms. Simplicity is the best rule to follow. Keep the ideas basic and simple.

The magician enters, bows, goes to his worktable, exhibits his tools, concocts his magic, bows, and departs. What kind of magician is he? Glad! Glad and happy and very confident— knowing his business, knowing he is giving the audience pleasure.

The boy who did this pantomime had a great deal of fun with it, because what he chose to do was simple and well-defined. The music was gay and rollicking, "The Glockenspiel Gavotte." He walked away from the stage feeling enormously successful, although he was not particularly talented.

If the children leave this lesson feeling confident about their choices of ideas and how well they are working out, their rehearsal periods at home will show improvement next time.

Lesson 12

1. You have now had a chance to rehearse your record pantomime.
2. Here are some questions you should have asked yourself during your rehearsal:
    a. Am I keeping the correct time? Am I going too fast or too slow for the beat of the music?
    b. Am I using my face and body to express my thoughts and feelings?
    c. Am I using my hands expressively?
    d. Do my feet move quickly and gracefully?
    e. Am I telling the story clearly with movement?
    f. Am I moving in such a way that my audience can see my actions clearly?
3. When you do your pantomime today for your teacher, she will correct you on these points.
4. Today is the day to ask all the questions that are in your mind concerning your idea and how you will express it.
5. Try to make your pantomime so good that every change of rhythm in the record is interpreted correctly by you.
6. Try to give characterization to your improvisation.
    a. What type of person is your character?
    b. Do you walk as he would walk?
    c. Do you react to things as he would?
    d. What are his mannerisms?
7. If someone else is in the improvisation, someone imaginary, work hard to convince us he is present.
8. If your character is funny, don't be afraid to be funny.
9. If your character is sad or mad, don't be afraid to be sad or mad.
10. One of the aims of this exercise is to enable you to relax in front of an audience. So have fun doing your musical pantomime. Be sure to put a lot of spirit and vitality into everything you do.

Assignment for next lesson:
Continue to practice and develop your record pantomime. It is by
no means ready to perform. By next lesson you should have added
some new touches to it. Check this sheet during your rehearsal, and
make sure you are doing everything in Items 2 and 6.

LESSON 13

Setting Our Business

We think of this lesson as a sort of technical rehearsal, one in
which we try to iron out any technical problems the child has.
Although this exercise is essentially a pantomime in the sense
that it is primarily one of movement and expression, we permit
him to use furniture and a costume aid or prop if he chooses.
However, these must be kept at an absolute minimum. An
umbrella, parasol, a fan, a crutch, a cane, or a flower is sometimes an inspiration, motivating the child to use his body more
expressively.

Setting the Stage

The teacher should have no elaborate lighting problems. The
lights she uses at each lesson will be sufficient if she feels that
the lighting has been adequate all along. The furniture that the
children use at each lesson should be set and permanent. It
should be part of the stage equipment. This is a discipline
which inspires confidence. In most cases, because of the short-
age of time, I do not draw the curtain on each pantomime.
Rather, I ask the children as they come onstage to set the

furniture exactly as they wish to use it and then give the audience an explanation of what they are going to do before they begin. We start today to rehearse this opening explanation so that the children will feel more confident and improve it as time goes on. Then I ask them to draw an imaginary curtain upon themselves when they have finished and count to five slowly before they conclude with a short bow from the waist down.

As mentioned previously, the teacher will have to supervise the placing of furniture so that we will be sure the audience has a good view of all the action. The business must be absolutely set at this rehearsal. Most children need this assistance. Occasionally a child will surprise you with an uncanny sense of staging, keeping well-aware of the audience every minute. But this is unusual in a beginner.

Keeping Open

The children will learn the body positions and stage areas in the next quarter. They will learn how to keep their bodies open to the audience. Since they have had little instruction in these fundamentals up until now, they must be encouraged to keep aware of the audience and make the action simple and open so that "we can see everything that you do. This will keep our interest alive."

A hungry boy who goes through the simple action of coming home from school and making a simple snack sets his table Center Stage, stands behind it, and prepares his food facing the audience. So does the girl who wants to surprise her mother by baking a cake. Often the children visualize their own kitchens, and we have to change things a little to suit our purpose. A girl who sneaks into her mother's bedroom, sits at her vanity, and borrows her makeup should do this in a full front position with the vanity parallel to the footlights, rather than in a profile position facing Right or Left Stage. We simply apply common sense to these minor problems.

More Than We Can Chew

Sometimes a child tries to stretch his action over too many locales. We encounter this tendency very often. It is a hangover from the world of make-believe he has just recently left or is just about to leave—the world where he could be anything or anywhere at a moment's notice! We understand this and tenderly encourage him to modify his idea rather than permit it to get involved with too much clutter. If he goes from home to the office, we designate these two definite areas and work within their confines.

The teacher renders her greatest service at this level of training by instilling in the young performer the rudiments of a basic and simple early discipline.

Work simply, boys and girls. Do not invent too many things to do that you cannot carry out successfully. After you have chosen two or three basic actions, work on them over and over again at home. This is how a good actor rehearses. He does not change his actions and expressions at every rehearsal up until the opening of the play. He may experiment for a little while until he finds what he wants to do, and then he starts working and building these actions into something permanent.

Before the children leave class today the teacher asks them to continue to work on the opening remarks that introduce each individual pantomime to the audience.

Remember, children, to state your remarks clearly, firmly, and confidently. After I have called your name, I want you to go onstage and arrange your furniture the way you want it. Then come to Downstage Center and tell the audience the type of character you are, the setting, and what you are going to do. Mention also the title of your music. Work on this introduction many times before your next lesson so that you will be very confident of your choice of words. This confidence will carry over to us—the audience—and we will become very enthusiastic to see what you are going to show us.

Lesson 13

1. Today is your technical rehearsal.
2. Technical comes from the word TECHNIQUE, which is a method of performance in any art, the technical skill of an art.
3. The art we are concerned with is drama.
4. Technique must be gained by practice.
5. We are practicing our exercise, our record pantomime, so that we will become skilled in doing it.
6. This is the last day that you should make any changes in your action.
7. From today, everything that you do in your pantomime should be set.
8. Work today on your introduction.
9. First, give your record to your teacher or whoever plays the record.
10. Then set your stage. Put furniture where you want it.
11. Then walk to Downstage Center and introduce yourself.
12. Tell the audience the idea of your pantomime and title of your record.
13. Do your pantomime; climax it thoroughly; bow to your audience.

Assignment for next lesson:

Practice your pantomime daily. Practice will make it clearer and more perfect. Try to make your performance as professional as possible. A professional person is positively sure of everything he does.

LESSON 14

Polishing Our Pantomimes

We call this lesson the first dress rehearsal. We hope that we have ironed out most of the technical wrinkles by this time and that the children will rehearse from now on with the audience in mind. Company is coming!

Rehearsing with Our Audience in Mind

Today the teacher should strive for a quick-moving and effective presentation. She must encourage the children to introduce their pantomimes clearly and arrange the necessary furniture in a businesslike, professional way.

They must rehearse today in the order they will follow at the performance. I usually rely on alphabetical order unless there is some other sequence it would seem more reasonable to follow. It is important that everyone know who precedes him so that he has an idea of what furniture is being used previously and can arrange his own quickly and efficiently.

Getting Closer to Our Character

Today the teacher must encourage the children to project their characters beyond the stage.

Make the character you are *bigger* so that the audience will understand him better. Since we do not have words, or dialogue, to help us express our characters, our movements and expressions have got to be bigger, projected more, a little bit larger than life. Remember, in order to do this you must concentrate. Think hard—for all the time you are moving to the music, thinking about your business, projecting your personality, you are *acting!*

The teacher will find that it will be more difficult to achieve good concentration with the eight- and nine-year-olds if she does not start working on this element early in the rehearsals. Along the way they must be prepared for an audience, so that when the big day arrives, they will not be totally distracted. I do this by mentioning quite frequently that the parents are coming to see them and by rehearsing with the rest of the class sitting in a tight group, close to the stage, so that the person performing will get the feel of the onlooker, the audience.

Children, try to make everything that you do today exceptionally sharp and *keen.* Keen means to be accurate and eager— just right! Keen means to feel things deeply and intensely. When you give your introductions, smile at the audience keenly so that we see the smile set deeply in your eyes. Feel your pleasure at seeing the people who have come to see you keenly. The same goes for everything that you feel—happiness, gaiety, sadness, tiredness, or whatever your character dictates.

Lesson 14

1. Today is your first dress rehearsal day.
2. Make good use of the time that you have left to give a first-rate performance.
3. Try to imagine that your teacher and fellow students are a large audience that you are trying to please and entertain to the best of your ability.
4. From now on rehearse as if you were performing.
5. Make a note of all your teacher's comments, and try to be PERFECT for the final dress rehearsal next week.
6. If you have any problems, you should take care of them today.
7. All of your technical problems should have been solved last

week, but if you are still having some troubles with props or furniture, be sure to solve them today.
8. Next week will be your final dress rehearsal. It should be just like a performance.

Assignment for next lesson:
Continue to practice your pantomime. Make sure to invite your parents and those who wish to see your performance. Get an accurate account of the people who are coming and be prepared to tell your teacher this number at the next lesson.

LESSON 15

Last-Minute Pointers

Today is our final dress rehearsal. We start our program as quickly as possible so that we can get a fairly accurate timing on it for the performance next week. This is important if we have subsequent classes all preparing performances. We must start on time and dismiss on time, allowing some moments for questions parents may want to ask when it is over.

The teacher checks equipment and furniture before the lesson begins. Sometimes props we have grown accustomed to having around for several weeks suddenly disappear at a crucial moment.

Sighs of Satisfaction
She is particularly anxious to see the improvements the child has made on his introduction and pantomime. The biggest sign of improvement is the degree to which the child seems

able to switch his concentration and involvement into the record pantomime and to sustain it. Sustaining his character as he moves through his business while concentrating on the mood and tempo of the music indicates various degrees of intelligence, imagination, maturity, physical and mental coordination, sensitivity, emotional depth, and *talent!*

The teacher sighs pleasurably as she sees the children moving through their pantomimes with happy assurance. Watching the really keen ones will produce an extra stab of exhilaration. But it is the sense of accomplishment, the happy success the child feels that is our biggest achievement. Creating his own idea and bringing it to fruition, preparing the stage for it and introducing it, getting it off successfully, enjoying the triumph of it, and then recalling it as a memory from which will spring other successes—this is what we want for him!

Last-Minute Details

No matter how simple the lighting setup is, the teacher makes sure today that this is what she will be working with for the performance. If she has decided to dim the houselights, she must do so at this rehearsal. Nothing must occur at the performance that the children are not technically prepared for, unless it be an accident! This applies to the use of the curtain also.

During this lesson the teacher should get as accurate a number as possible of those who are going to attend the performance. This is important to the overall success of the program. If there are ample seats for a large crowd, then there is no need for concern. If the room is small and seating space limited, the teacher should ask each child how many from his family are attending and prepare accordingly. If seating space will be severely limited, she should have stipulated at the beginning of this project, the number of guests each child is permitted to bring. The children should leave class today having a very clear understanding of the audience seating arrangement so that they will know what to tell their parents.

Pretend You Perform

Everything we do today should be carried out as much in the spirit of the performance as possible. The teacher assures the children where the phonograph will be and who will be playing it. I usually take care of this duty myself. They must know, too, exactly where they are to sit.

> Come to Downstage Center with quickness and enthusiasm. Welcome your audience with a warm smile. Tell them about your pantomime—what you are going to do. Remember, children, all the time and effort you have put into these rehearsals is going to end at the next lesson, when you present your ideas to an audience. So enjoy this moment. Your pantomime is the story of an experience which you are going to share with your audience. This enjoyment, this pleasure, is a reciprocal thing which the audience returns to you—reacting to your story in movement, appreciating it.

After the teacher has generated a little excitement and they are wriggling in their seats, anxious to begin—and a certain kind of quiet settles over all—she reaches for her roll book and starts with Nancy Adams.

Nancy eagerly comes to Downstage Center and breathlessly begins: "My name is Nancy Adams, and I have chosen for my music "The Age of Gold Polka" by Shostakovich. In this pantomime I am a country hick with a knapsack on my back, seeking my city cousin. I have never been to the city before, and the noise and confusion frighten and bewilder me. Skyscrapers, automobiles—What are they?—I have never seen them before. . . ."

Lesson 15

1. Today is your final dress rehearsal.
2. Ask your teacher about anything that is troubling you.
3. Tell your teacher the number of parents, relatives, and friends who are coming to see your performance. Your teacher must know this in order to assure them of seats.
4. Next week remember to be prompt. The performance must start on time.
5. Don't forget your record!
6. Don't forget important costume essentials and props!
7. Don't forget your parents!

Assignment for next lesson:

Rehearse your pantomime at least once each day, as you did last week. Remember to be prompt next week. The performance must start on time. Clear any last-minute details with your teacher. Don't forget important costume essentials and props.

LESSON 16

Performance of Musical Pantomime

Today is our performance lesson. The teacher thinks of it as a learning experience, and she has not permitted the idea of a performance to take on too much magnitude throughout the rehearsal period.

On with the Show

As parents and relatives file in the teacher checks each child to see if he is present and his record is intact—not cracked or broken since he left the house this morning. These things do happen! The children find their seats and get settled with records and props. When everyone is here, we are ready to begin.

The teacher feels that she must talk to the parents for a short while about the exercise they are about to witness. She introduces herself and begins:

Today is my opportunity to meet you parents, relatives, and friends. We have been waiting for you to visit us and have been working on this exercise with you in mind. We know that you mothers are especially anxious to visit the class, even though I'm sure you already know what you are going to see today. If the children have attacked this assignment correctly, they should have spent much time working on it at home. We would like to ask you in for a visit more often, but we feel that a constant stream of visitors is very distracting and sometimes inhibits the class. But we are so glad you are here with us today.

We spent the first two lessons relaxing and getting to know one another better. Then we had some improvisations to make sure that we understood what the basis of acting is. After that we spent some time learning the elements of good speech. At this level we are concerned primarily with diction and articulation— making sure that we know what to do with our articulators: our lips, tongue, and teeth.

And then we came to this assignment, the record pantomime. We choose this exercise for many reasons, but most important because it insures a successful first experience with an audience and teaches us a lot about each child. It also gives the child an opportunity to pour much of his power of imagination and observation into his own creation over an extended period of time.

Today, as you watch the children go through these pantomimes, look for the individuality of each and particularly for the way he prepares to present his.

After our program has ended, please feel free to ask me any question you may have in mind.

And now, since we are ready to go, let's begin, shall we? First on our roll is Nancy Adams!

We hope that, during this first meeting with the parents, the teacher will observe them as closely as they scrutinize her. She certainly can find out much about each child in this way— mainly how much encouragement he gets at home in pursuing the study of drama. She should honestly make any recommendations for the child to the parents if she thinks it necessary. If she wishes, the teacher may also give a brief outline of the material to be covered in the approaching semester.

Lesson 16

1. Today is your performance day!
2. Check your record and props.
3. Clear any last-minute details with your teacher.
4. Relax! Have fun! Enjoy your audience!
5. Give a good performance.

Assignment for next lesson:

Next week we begin to learn that acting is an art that requires discipline. Now that you have learned the importance of poise, confidence, voice and speech, and good, free body movement, you will begin to act with others in scenes. Working with scripts and learning to know the stage areas and how to use them is exciting fun. So be on time next week, ready to start the new semester. Bring lots of pep and enthusiasm with you, and don't forget to bring a pencil.

PART V

Exploring the Stage

LESSON 17

A Bit About the Stage

An Art and a Discipline

Drama is an art. Taken in its entirety, it encompasses several sister arts. The playwriting, acting, directing, costuming, scenery and lighting combine to make it, in the opinion of many, the most consummate and exciting of all the art forms. If we become involved with it and grow to love it, we are willing to accept the discipline that it demands. Through discipline the actor trains his body to become a willing instrument of his total expression.

Exploring the Stage

When a teacher introduces a child to the rudiments of ballet or the piano, from the start he imposes certain disciplinary exercises as part of the learning practice to develop an individual technique. Without these, there would be no basis for communication or rapport. So it must be with drama, especially if the child is to have a continued interest from year to year. He must develop step by step. We have spent the last sixteen lessons acquainting the child with the dramatic situation and helping him to relax in it. Now is the time, before we attempt the discipline that a script requires—with blocking and movement and memorization of lines—to introduce him to the different areas of the stage.

We do this now, before we start our work with a script, because:

1. He is ready for it.
2. It makes him more conscious of his body.
3. He begins to realize how his body is related to the stage.
4. The stage will take on a different meaning for him.
5. He becomes more aware of a director.
6. The play script will take on a definition for him.
7. This will be the springboard for further pleasant experiences in drama. They will not be vague.
8. He feels that drama is serious, that we are not just fooling around.

Think for a moment, boys and girls, about how it is when we are learning something new. When we first learned all the facts about a football field or a baseball field or a hockey field, we were told that they each have divisions or locations that are important to the rules of the game. Certain plays that vary in significance take place on certain locations on the field. The field has to be divided in such a way as to give the game a form that we enjoy watching. So it is with drama. Until today we haven't concerned ourselves with the serious rules that the stage imposes on good actors, but they are there and they always apply to a normal stage that faces the audience and is separated from it by a curtain. Now I am going to tell you more about our stage and its divisions, or areas.

The teacher then distributes a sheet upon which is a diagram of the stage and its areas and another indicating their abbreviations:

The teacher explains that the diagram is based on the actor's right and left as he stands onstage facing the audience. She explains each area as she moves from one to the other. I

UP RIGHT	UP CENTER	UP LEFT
RIGHT STAGE	CENTER STAGE	LEFT STAGE
DOWN RIGHT	DOWN CENTER	DOWN LEFT

AUDIENCE

UR	URC	UC	ULC	UL
R	RC	C	LC	L
DR	DRC	DC	DLC	DL

AUDIENCE

usually start at the center. If the stage is very small, she may, if she chooses, omit the Right Center and the Left Center areas entirely from the discussion and actual usage. I like to include them in the diagram, because in a few years hence the children who continue to study drama will learn that there are actually fifteen areas, and they might as well learn them now.

Why We Have Stage Areas

As she moves from area to area the teacher may give a little of the history of how stage areas came to be:

> Of course, we already know that the stage has a history. The early Greeks sat on a hillside and watched the actors in a kind of hollowed-out pit below. As the centuries advanced, so did the stage. For a while the stage was a church or large cathedral. In some places it was a roughly built platform in a market square or the courtyard of an inn, with people looking on from the galleries. Then it grew to be important enough to have its own house—the theater—and it was at this time that stage directions came into being. They are derived from an early period when the stage was *raked*, or sloped upward toward the back. Any advancing movement toward the audience is said to proceed Downstage, while any retiring movement away from the audience is termed a movement Upstage. In these early days many important scenes were played in the Downstage areas, and many of these early traditions are still in use in the theater today.

The teacher continues to tell the children how one should turn onstage, how he should be aware of the difference in the upstage and downstage foot and hand and start on the upstage foot whenever possible. She explains how he must use his upstage hand so that he does not cover himself or his action. She demonstrates here so that the children fully understand this. It goes without saying that there are many, many acting technique rules that we cannot include here. They are too many and too burdensome for the children at this point, but they grasp the most obvious very easily and are captivated practicing them.

If there is time after the explanation of the stage, I suggest a simple pantomime by each child. As he does this alone onstage I urge him to think—for the first time—of his actions onstage, as well as of himself. "Where am I now onstage? Where am I going?" At the same time he must try not to betray his thoughts to the audience. He must not talk—just move.

Here are some suggestions for pantomimes:

1. A woman comes into a cluttered room and decides to straighten it up.
2. A boy arrives at camp with his luggage. He enters his room and starts to unpack.
3. A woman decides to rearrange the furniture.
4. A vacuum sweeper salesman gives a demonstration.
5. A man is deciding where to hang a picture.
6. A girl gives dancing lessons.
7. A boy decorates his game room for a party.
8. A girl shuts the blinds, prepares to take a nap.

After this exercise we prepare to leave the class with our stage directions neatly intact. We are going to learn them carefully for next lesson.

Remember to learn the stage areas, keeping in mind that they apply to the actor's right and left as he stands onstage. Next lesson I will give stage directions, and *you will follow.*

Lesson 17

1. It may seem that you have spent a lot of time studying acting, but you have really spent very little time—for sixteen lessons is not much time to spend on learning. You spend about thirty-five hours a week in school. Did you ever look at it this way?
2. Today we are going to learn some of the basic rules that an actor must follow if he is to become a good actor.
3. For many, many years actors have had to follow rules, just as good football players must do.
4. The stage is divided into sections we call AREAS.
5. Your teacher will give you a diagram of the stage areas and explain these terms.

6. The director, who tells the actor where to go onstage, knows these areas and also expects the actor to know them. You must get to know them as soon as possible, so you and your teacher-director will work well together on your scenes.
7. After the explanation of stage areas your teacher will have you do some short pantomimes.
8. Relax and enjoy your exercises.

Assignment for next lesson:

Study your stage diagram sheet carefully for next lesson. Make a neat copy of it and bring this to class next lesson. We are going to make sure that we know where all the areas are.

LESSON 18

Stage Areas and Body Positions

The lesson today is devoted exclusively to the stage and its areas. The teacher must discover who finds stage directions easy or difficult. She asks each child to come to Center Stage. Then she may call directions to make sure he has studied his stage diagram, or she may ask each child to locate them himself and tell us what they are as he comes to them. If the class is small, I would suggest doing this several times with each child until he is sure of them.

Important Stage Techniques

We mentioned in the last lesson calling attention to the use of the upstage hand and foot. This simply means that if a person is going to make a cross from Left to Right Stage or vice versa or from Up Right to Down Left or Down Right to Up Left, he should start with a small step on the foot closest to the upstage area. Doing this prevents him from covering his body and presents a clearer, more aesthetically pleasing view to the audience. As he crosses from area to area today we urge him to use his upstage foot first, stopping and correcting him if he does not.

The teacher may take a few moments to demonstrate here the use of the upstage hand. She may use a prop such as a telephone or a letter. She explains that an actor usually handles objects with the upstage hand whenever it is possible. If he is handling several things at a time, then he must carefully work out his stage business. I usually demonstrate the use of the upstage hand and foot by having the children watch me as I say some simple lines. I stand in a right or left profile position on Right or Left Stage and ask one of the children to stand on the opposite side of the stage holding a paper or letter. Without much thought to character, I ask the children to observe me as I do this exercise two ways: first incorrectly, then correctly. First I say, "Give me the letter." (*Cross in using upstage foot first, extending upstage hand.*) "I said, 'Give it to me.'" (*Cross in again with hand still extended.*) "Did you hear me? I said, '*Give me the letter.*'" The child with the letter hands it to me with the upstage hand. The children easily notice the difference in the correct and incorrect version.

Body Positions

After she is sure they have grasped the idea of the stage areas being allocated to the actor's right and left and know where they are and how to get to them, the teacher introduces the children to the various body positions an actor can take onstage.

She distributes a sheet with this diagram:

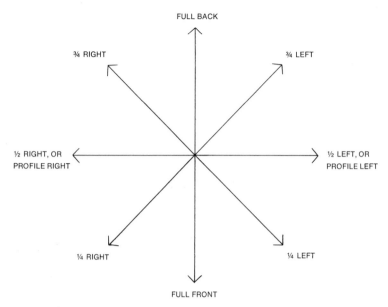

After the teacher demonstrates the various body positions, she calls on each child to come onstage, and we do them individually. She is careful to explain that no matter where the actor stands onstage, these body positions always receive the same terms or labels.

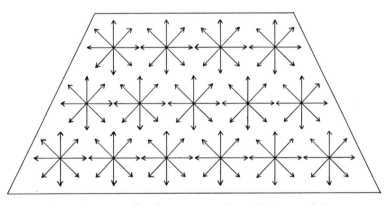

We leave class with this material tucked carefully in our notebooks.

We learn that we can assume attitudes and poses as we shift be-
tween the restrictions of the eight body positions.

Next week we are going to do stage directions combined with body positions. Please review often everything we have covered in today's lesson. Be ready to assume all body positions onstage at our next lesson.

Lesson 18

1. Today your teacher will collect your copy of the stage direction diagram.
2. Then she will ask each of you to come onstage and show the class how well you understand the chart.
3. She will ask you to CROSS to the individual areas. Cross is a term we use when taking or giving stage directions, such as XDR or XL. (*Cross Down Right or Cross Left*)
4. Then she will explain and demonstrate to you the various body positions an actor can assume while onstage.
5. If there is time your teacher will have you show her that you understand the positions. She will have you go onstage and do them.

Assignment for next lesson:

Study your body position chart carefully. Restudy your stage area diagram. Next week we are going to take stage directions and body positions from our teacher.

LESSON 19

Review and Other Techniques

Today we do an exercise day devoted entirely to the disciplinary task of making sure the child understands body positions and stage areas. He learns by doing himself and by watching others. If the class is small, the teacher can run through a series of stage directions several times with each child.

Let's Exercise

These directions should be basic and simple. I make the first set deliberately easy. I ask the child to:

XC
Take a full front position
XDC
Take a full back position
XUC
Take a profile right
XUR
Take a profile left
XUL
Take a ¼ position right
XR
Take a ¼ position left
XDL
Take a ¾ position right
XUR
Take a ¼ position left
XL
Take a ¼ position right
XDR
Exit

An exercise such as the above gets the child in position for his next move. At this level this is necessary for most children. We could permit him to cross from one area to another without taking the body position first, but then he could develop the bad habit of making sloppy turns and sliding into position. As each child does this exercise the others are asked to notice if he starts his cross with the upstage foot first. We notify him if he does not. These lessons on stage movement are usually accompanied with much demonstration from the teacher. She spends this lesson going over these simple directions until she is certain each child understands them. I am constantly amazed at how quickly the eight- and nine-year-olds absorb them. But they can forget them just as easily if we do not put them into immediate practice.

If there is time and she feels that the children can incorporate everything at this lesson, the teacher may give directions without body positions. Just ask the children to cross from one area to another *without* telling them to take a body position which always gets them ready for the next move. Directions such as these present a few problems. They usually lead to discussions of how one turns onstage (toward the audience), the size of steps one takes (normal), and so forth. The explanation of curved crosses or approaches is useful here, too: A curved approach keeps the actor open to the audience, softens a cross, and shows off a costume:

Important items to be gotten from this lesson are these:
1. The stage has a terminology.
2. All people concerned vitally with the play, especially actors, directors, and playwrights, must learn this terminology.
3. An actor must develop a whole visual technique.

4. Acting technique is developed through practice.

5. His body and how he moves onstage are very important.
Before the class breaks the teacher tells the children that next week they are going to take her place for a while.

I want you to prepare a list of directions very much like the ones I have given you today. You may select another member of the class and give him the directions you have written. Be prepared to correct him if he makes a mistake. Remember, you are to look upon these exercises with the eye of a director. Write at least twelve directions.

Lesson 19

1. Today your teacher is going to make absolutely certain that you know the meaning of the following terms:

Areas	Full front
Positions	¼ Right or Left
Onstage	Profile Right or Left
Offstage	¾ Right or Left
Upstage	Full back
Downstage	Open up
The wings	Turn in
The apron	Turn out
Playing space	Upstage foot
Curved approaches	Cross

2. Then she is going to give you directions, telling you to take certain positions and cross to certain areas.

3. Remember that onstage, when an actor goes to a particular area, he always uses the term "cross."

4. Your teacher is going to give you directions that will sound something like this: "XC, take a ¼ position Right, XDR, take a profile Left."

5. After everyone in class has gone through directions like the one above, your teacher will explain your assignment for next lesson.

Assignment for next lesson:

You are to bring in a list of twelve stage directions which are to read like Number 4 in today's lesson. You are to write these neatly on a piece of paper, and you are going to read them to another pupil who will do the movements that you read onstage. Someone else will give his directions to you. Everyone must read and take directions.

LESSON 20

Students Give Directions

This lesson is devoted entirely to repeating the stage direction exercises. This time it is the students who call them. The teacher urges each member of the class to observe carefully and patiently each person taking directions, no matter how confident he himself feels of knowing the material.

Remember, class, aside from his voice, the actor has only one instrument—his body. He must train his body to do his will, as a good athlete does. The stage, with its various rules and its terminology, imposes a discipline on the actor, just as the piano does upon a pianist. We must learn the rules.

Today we are going to give and take stage directions, just as we did last week. Only today, you, the students, will become the directors. Every one of you must watch carefully and notice if the person onstage is doing everything correctly. It is important to recognize mistakes. You will learn from watching the mistakes of others. The person giving directions must watch the person onstage to see if he starts a cross with the upstage foot. The person giving directions must call them out in a clear, firm voice. The person taking directions must be sure to relax, stand straight, walk well, hold his head erect, and always start on the upstage foot. The class will spend most of the lesson on this, because it is so very important that we learn to move well onstage.

Let's Observe Each Other Closely

Both teacher and class become alert observers of the exercises today. She interrupts to correct a mistake whenever necessary and demonstrates to clarify a point wherever possible.

As we wind up our lesson today the teacher gives the class time to prepare for next lesson's assignment:

Next week you are going to give an improvisation with someone else. Two people will work together. I will give you time today to select a partner and work on your idea. The idea must be a good one for stage movement. The class is going to criticize mistakes. We are going to notice whether you started on the upstage foot, how you stood, walked, and crossed. Of course, you are going to talk to each other, so use your best voice. You are going to pick your partner and your idea today and think about how you are going to move onstage at our next lesson. Be sure that your improvisation takes place in one locale, like a room. Have an idea that has a beginning, middle, and end. Be sure to think of a good idea with interesting movement. Think about it a lot before the next lesson.

If the class has an odd number, the teacher should assign three to work together or have one person do two improvisations with two different people. She should make sure that the ideas they are working with are good. If they aren't, she should supply good ones herself. The idea must be one that naturally motivates movement, such as, "Two girls decide to tidy up their room."

Lesson 20

1. Today we are going to give and take stage directions.
2. Everyone must watch carefully and notice if the person onstage is doing everything correctly.
3. It is important to recognize mistakes. You will learn from watching the mistakes of others.
4. The person taking directions must watch the person onstage to see if he starts to cross with the upstage foot.
5. The person giving directions must call them out in a clear, firm voice.
6. The person taking directions must be sure to relax, stand straight, walk well, hold his head erect, and always start on the upstage foot.
7. The class will spend most of the lesson on this, because it is very important that we learn to move well onstage.
8. About ten minutes before the class is over your teacher will explain next lesson's assignment to you and give you a few minutes to pick a partner and discuss your ideas.

Assignment for next lesson:

Next lesson you are to give an improvisation with someone else. Two people will be working together. Your teacher will give you time today to pick a partner and select your idea. The idea must be a good one for movement. The class is going to criticize mistakes. We are going to notice if you started on the upstage foot, how you stood, walked, and crossed. Of course, you are going to talk to each other, so use your best voice. You are going to pick your partner and your idea today. Think about how you are going to move onstage at the next lesson. Be sure that your improvisation takes place in one locale, like a room. Have an idea with a beginning, middle, and end. Be sure to think of some good ideas for interesting movement.

LESSON 21

Review with Pantomime

We hope the improvisations today will improve with our study of stage movement. The student, through the study of stage directions and body movements, should begin to realize that movement on the stage must be economical and mean something. The first improvisations were cluttered with extraneous movement. We hope these will be different.

The ideas need not be striking or original. In fact, it is better if they are simple and basic to movement. The teacher stresses that both characters should have an equal amount of movement. Two people may decide to get a meal. One starts to cook; the other sets the table. Each makes several crosses to get the items he needs. Both people taking part in the improvisation come to the front of the class. While one person is explaining the idea and where the scene takes place the other person should be getting the stage ready.

Pantomime to Improve

The class is prepared to criticize, using the same standards as in the two previous lessons. We are not looking for directorial errors, since this improvisation has no director. We closely watch each character, what he does, how he moves and crosses, the use of his upstage hand and foot. Does he keep his action open to the audience? How does he turn? Do we understand what is taking place? Is his pantomime authentic—that is, pantomime in regard to props and furniture we have to imagine to be there? We cannot go off on too much of a tangent here regarding pantomime, but we hope it will be well thought out and believable.

We spend the entire period doing the improvisations and discussing them. If the teacher is not satisfied with certain movements, she demonstrates how they should be done. She constantly asserts how important it is for the actor to do things onstage that look good to the audience. The audience likes to be pleased with this constantly moving picture on stage.

Before we leave class the teacher urges everyone to go over his material on stage movement, review what we have recently done from time to time, and be prepared to block a short scene at the next lesson. Pencils are very necessary.

Lesson 21

1. Today you are going to perform your improvisations for your teacher and the class.
2. Both people taking part in this improvisation must come to the front of the class.
3. While one person is explaining the idea and where the scene takes place the other person should be getting the stage ready.
4. Make sure that your set is right before you start your scene.
5. Don't crowd your stage.
6. Make good use of the available furniture.
7. Remember to use all the rules for good stage movement that we have discussed.
8. Remember especially to always start with the upstage foot.
9. Everyone will do the improvisation once.
10. If some need correction and there is time, we will do them twice.
11. Pay close attention. Criticize fairly. What you learn with these improvisations will affect your work next lesson.

Assignment for next lesson:

Review all the work you have done with stage movement during the past five lessons. Next lesson we will BLOCK a scene. Be sure to bring a pencil with you.

PART VI

Handling the Script

LESSON 22

Reading and Blocking

Exercises with Scripts

Exercise

The scene is the office of the principal of an elementary school. The PRINCIPAL, PUPIL, *and* TEACHER *may be played by either a boy or a girl. The* PUPIL *has been called to the office, because his teacher found him disobeying a school rule. The* PRINCIPAL *is seated at his desk when the* PUPIL *enters.*

PRINCIPAL (*looking up from desk*): Good morning. You're Pat Anderson, is that right?

PUPIL: Yes, sir (ma'am).

PRINCIPAL: Well, come in. Sit down here. (*Gestures to chair.*) It's a little early to be getting into trouble today, isn't it? Your teacher tells me you broke out of the recess line before it reached the schoolyard. Is this the story?

PUPIL: Yes, sir (ma'am). It is. I dropped my ball and chased it.

PRINCIPAL: Your teacher says you were tossing your ball in the air the minute you left the school building. You know you shouldn't do this until you reach the recess yard.

PUPIL: No, sir (ma'am). My ball just fell.

PRINCIPAL: Tell your teacher I would like to see her (him). (PUPIL *goes out to get* TEACHER. *They both re-enter.*)

PRINCIPAL: Miss Smith, Pat tells me he (she) just dropped the ball. I understood you to say he (she) was tossing it.

TEACHER: That's right. (TEACHER *crosses to window.*) He (she) started from the door over there and kept it up all along the walk until he (she) dropped it. (TEACHER *turns back into room.*)

PRINCIPAL: It seems that Pat can't remember exactly what did happen.

TEACHER: Yes, I know. He (she) couldn't remember exactly whether he (she) hit me with an eraser or not, either.

PRINCIPAL: Well, this is getting serious! Throwing erasers, eh? What have you got to say about this?

PUPIL: All I can say is that the ball fell, and the eraser slipped out of my hand. Sounds funny, but it's true.

PRINCIPAL: Oh, it sounds funny, does it? (*He crooks finger.*) Come with me, young man (young lady), and we'll see how funny it really is. (*He crosses to opposite end of room. Gestures for* PUPIL *to follow.* TEACHER *looks at* PRINCIPAL. *Exits.*)

Exercise

Three children appear in this scene. The parts of Jo *and* PAT *may be played by boys or girls. The scene is the living room of* Jo's *home. A party is being planned.*

ANNE: You know, Jo, I think it's swell of your mom to let us have the party here.

PAT: Didn't she even raise one little objection?

Jo: Oh, sure—she warned me what would happen if we raised the roof.

ANNE: That never crossed my mind. Come to think of it . . .

PAT: Say—that's a terrific stereo you have. Can we use it? (*Crosses to stereo.*)

Jo: I'm not sure. I'll ask. My dad has a great record collection.

ANNE: And the piano will be perfect, too. Arabella Henry can play it for us. (*Crosses to piano.*)

PAT: Oh, no! What for? Who wants to hear her play? Tum Tum Da Dum Dum Da Doo Da Doo Da Doo. Every Friday at Assembly. What do we need all the music for, anyway?

ANNE: Dancing, dope!

PAT: Who can dance? Name one person in our class who can dance.

JO: Me. I can dance. The _____ (name of popular dance). That's my specialty. (*Demonstrates.*)

PAT: Fine. You can _____ by yourself. I doubt if anyone else can do it.

ANNE: Oh, I don't know about that (*she tries a* _____. *Jo joins her.*)

PAT: Well, I can always sing. (*He or she takes a position and starts to sing.*)

ANNE: Hey, that's an idea. Why don't we have amateur night? Arabella Henry can play the piano—

JO: Yes,—and Ellsworth Morgan plays the oboe.

PAT (*over near window*): Here come Dick and Linda. They'll have lots of ideas.

Blocking

After the teacher distributes the scenes to the students, she tells them that they are going to *block* the scene today and makes sure that they understand the meaning of this term.

For the past several lessons we have been learning certain basic, simple rules that the stage demands every actor to know. Actually, learning these rules makes acting easier for the actor and the director. Now, with a script in your hands, and a pencil, you will see how you apply these rules. To *block* a scene means to give action to the printed words by giving the actors directions in movement. This lifts the play from the printed page and brings it to life. The director is in charge of the blocking. He tells the actors where he wants them to go. He arranges the actors in groups onstage that make a pleasing picture. The actor must mark these directions on his script and learn them. He carries his script with him and rehearses with it in his hand until he is positive of his movement and actions, or business, as we call it in the theater. All this describes the term known as blocking.

Our Scripts Need Symbols

The teacher explains further that the word "cross" is represented by simply marking X on the script. R and L indicate Right and Left Stage. XR would mean cross Right, and so forth.

We intend to spend time perfecting simple actions, such as crosses, gestures, and turns. The two scenes included here for this purpose are deliberately devoid of emotional situations that provide impetus for much and varied movement. Each child may bring what he wants to these simple, stereotyped roles, but they purposely prevent extraneous clutter in movement. The teacher does not make this a difficult task. However, she does want the children to learn that there is a discipline here that insists they learn a fixed piece of business and do it the right way at every rehearsal. The scenes are short, and we can do them over and over again.

There are two ways to mark a script:

a. Write directions in the margin, and draw a line to the word where the action takes place.

Example

Rise ← ──────────────────────────────

RICH: Well, I'll be a monkey's uncle.⌐ I never thought

XR ← we'd find it. You're right, for sure. These are the three x's.
What do you know?⌐ I never thought I'd live to see
the day when I, personally, Richard Warren Hillsdale,
would be the discoverer of the secret of the old cave!

b. If the script is double-spaced, write the directions between the lines above the word where the action takes place.

Example

Rise

RICH: Well, I'll be a monkey's uncle.↓I never thought
we'd find it. You're right, for sure. These are the three x's.

XR

What do you know?↓ I never thought I'd live to see
the day when I, personally, Richard Warren Hillsdale,
would be the discoverer of the secret of the old cave!

Always be sure to underline the last few words of the speech
ahead of yours. This is called your *cue*. Of course, you must
underline your own speech, too. It helps you to learn your lines
more easily. Be careful to mark exactly what you are to do. If
your director wants you to walk while you are saying a line, you
must mark this in your script.

The teacher has them sketch a ground plan of the set somewhere on the back of the script. "A ground plan is a sort of
bird's-eye view of the set on which you will be acting," she
explains.

Be Sure of Your Blocking

Since these are scenes for practice and not presentation, they
are easily cast. Certain parts are interchangeable to suit the
class. Before we are finished with this exercise, some children
will have played all parts in both scenes. The scenes are very
short. We read them a few times before we block. Then we
begin. The children are urged to watch the first blocking carefully and to mark their scripts with the young actors who are
doing it for the first time. This saves time and sharpens concentration. The teacher saves herself many problems at a later
date if she makes them repeat the blocking several times today
until they are absolutely certain of the business. She insists
that any turn be made outward to the audience. She calls upon
everyone to do the scene at least once.

Before leaving, she tells the class: "We will do the scene
without a script next lesson. Learn your lines and every move

perfectly. Study your blocking carefully. You must be perfect when we meet again."

Lesson 22

1. Today we are going to BLOCK a scene. Your teacher will explain this word to you.
2. Be sure that you have your pencil ready for the blocking.
3. Use this symbol for a cross: X.
4. You may have a direction to cross Down Right. On your script it will look like this: XDR.
5. There are two ways to mark your script.
   a. You may write your directions on the margin of your script and draw a line to the word where the action takes place.
   b. If your script is double-spaced, you may write the directions between the lines above the word where the action takes place.
6. Underline your lines and the last few words of the speech ahead of yours.
7. Be careful to mark exactly what you are to do.
8. If the director wants you to walk while you are saying a line, you must mark this on your script.
9. Every play has what we call a ground plan of the set. Your teacher will give you your ground plan for the short scenes. Below is a sketch showing what a ground plan looks like:

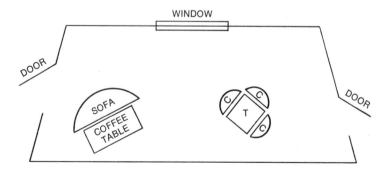

Assignment for next lesson:

Study your script blocking during the week. Learn every move. If you weren't sure of your business today, perfect it for next lesson. Underline your lines and cues. Bring a pencil to class next lesson— with a good eraser in case of additions.

LESSON 23

Making Sure

Because the scenes we use for blocking and marking the script are short, the children usually learn the lines for all six parts in this lesson. If some children did not get a chance to go through the blocking at the previous lesson, they should do so today. The teacher must make it a point to look at all scripts to make sure they understand what she is telling them to do. She checks for clarity and neatness. She repeats about under-lining lines and cues neatly and clearly.

Practice Makes Perfect

The scenes are simply blocked deliberately. Children are told to stand in clean-cut positions, without extraneous move-ment. We try to get them to feel the necessity of neat, clean crosses, standing in open positions, slipping gracefully from one position to another. They must come to understand the im-portance of economic use of gesture—gesture that means something.

The movement in the scene is entirely dependent upon the

judgment of the teacher. She may do whatever she wishes. The scenes are purposely simple and uncomplicated. The lines in the school scene are more motivated than in the other. We want the child to get around the stage incorporating the initial training in body technique he received at earlier lessons. Pay particular attention to his footwork and use of the upstage foot, his turning, his position when he speaks. But do not burden him with too much to do at first.

We urge the child to start to think about movement and character and voice.

Try today, boys and girls, to apply everything you have been learning since the beginning of your lessons to the characters and the scene you are playing. First of all, forget yourself, the old you. Leave that old you down there in the seat when you come onstage as someone else. This is the fun, the thrill, of acting. Then think about doing something with your voice. Remember, even though the actor uses a character voice at times, he always speaks within the framework of clear, understandable speech. It won't be hard for you to recall all the discussions we have had recently about stage movement, controlling our bodies, and keeping them related to the audience. We must apply all we know to these short scenes we are doing today.

Each child does the scene at least once. If there is time, he may do it two or three times. The teacher's biggest problem with this assignment is preventing it from becoming memorized and mechanical. She will have to give more supervision to eight- and nine-year-olds, especially in the area of script marking.

As class ends she tells the children that next lesson will be the final one we spend on our scene. With all lines learned and the blocking mastered, we will treat the next lesson as a mock performance.

Lesson 23

1. One rehearsal is never enough for the actor to become completely familiar with the blocking.
2. If you are in doubt about any of your directions, you should clear this up at once before you memorize the blocking.
3. Today, as you rehearse, try to move with feeling. Move slowly or quickly according to the feeling you have when you are speaking the lines.
4. Always start each movement with the upstage foot.
5. You must think, too, about the part you are playing.
6. How are you going to think about the character—as middle-aged or young or old?
7. What about the other characters? What is your relationship with them? How do you feel about them?
8. What about your voice? Remember, we spent some time on speech earlier this year.
   a. Use a clear, strong voice.
   b. Keep your lips moving. Don't be lazy.
   c. It is important for the tip of your tongue to be nimble and active.

Assignment for next lesson:

You should feel quite sure of your blocking after the rehearsal today. Next lesson we are going to pretend that we are presenting these scenes for an audience. It is the last day we will spend on them, so do the best work you possibly can. Remember, next lesson be absolutely certain of lines, movement, and character.

LESSON 24

We Play the Scene

The preceding quarter of eight lessons spent on stage movement culminates today in a short memorized scene which we repeat several times in class, each time with a different cast or with variations within the cast. This is not a performance, but we treat it as one and try to bring the excitement and energy to it that a performance demands.

The teacher dims the houselights. She may or may not use the curtain. The scene is short, and constant use of the curtain curtails the time we have; but if time permits, she may appoint a curtain puller.

Remember, Now We Are Actors

She encourages the class to inject performance quality into their acting today.

Let us present our scenes today as if an audience were out there breathlessly waiting for us to begin. First of all, we must make sure that our properties and furniture are exactly in the places they have been while we were rehearsing. This is extremely important for the actor—to be familiar with his surroundings. Then, as you begin your scene, you must think about nothing else but it and your acting. Do not worry about your lines and blocking today. If you have rehearsed them, they will come to you easily, and you will do them correctly during the performance. Try to imagine that you really are the student or teacher or principal or one of the children planning the party. Stand, sit, and think as your character would. Feel the way this character would feel in this situation. Remember to use that good voice. Feel relaxed and poised and confident today. Have fun with the scene and enjoy it!

Lesson 24

1. Today we are going to pretend that we are giving our scene for an audience.
2. This is called a performance, as you already know.
3. Before we start, make absolutely sure that your props and furniture are in the right place.
4. As you begin your scene think about nothing but the dramatic situation in which you are.
5. Do not worry about lines and blocking on the day of the performance. If you have rehearsed enough and learned them carefully, you will do them correctly during the performance.
6. Really imagine that you are the character.
7. Stand, sit, and think as your character would.
8. Speak with a clear, understandable voice.
9. Relax; be poised; have confidence.
10. Have fun today. Enjoy your scene.

Assignment for next lesson:

You have nothing to prepare for next lesson. Your teacher will give you scenes at the next lesson. These scenes, which will be presented for relatives and friends, will be our final assignment. Take a good rest and be prepared to work very hard on your scenes or playlets.

PART VII

Preparing the Play

Reading and Casting

Today our teacher comes to class with carefully selected scripts of playlets and scenes that she has been choosing for the past several weeks. This material has been chosen with the individual child in mind, as well as the size of the class and the time allotted to rehearse these scenes for presentation. Of course, we will present them at our last lesson. If this performance is an indication of the child's progress and final success in the course, it is even more an attestation to the teacher's talent and integrity.

Trimming Our Time

Of first importance is the dramatic material with which we will work for eight lessons. The playlets or scenes must be tailored to fit the size of the class. The teacher must be aware from the start that what takes a full period to rehearse at every lesson will perhaps play only ten or fifteen minutes. On the day of performance we do not want to be left with forty-five extra minutes that might have been utilized for two or three more scenes. On the other hand, if another class immediately succeeds this present one, with a new group of parents who have to be greeted and seated, we do not want the period to run overtime. What we choose must be neatly trimmed to fit within the

framework of the period at both rehearsal and performance—
leaving time afterward for any questions the parents may have.

What Shall We Play?

I feel that the teacher must keep her choice of material
simple. For most of the children this is still a new and experimental experience. Even though she may be encouraged and
pleased by their progress, she will create greater problems for
herself by choosing material that is too difficult or too long. I
have found that very short playlets or scenes from longer plays
that have an episodic quality play more successfully. I avoid
selecting plays with large casts, where the distribution of lines
is strewn over twelve or eighteen characters. This prevents the
average child from establishing a sense of characterization,
developing his concentration, and enjoying the enacting of a
tight dramatic situation.

A teacher can be the most experimental with a small group,
say four to six, because she has more time for suggestions and
rehearsal. With a class of eight to twelve or more, I generally
try to use scenes or playlets with four or six people and double-
cast. This is good for both the teacher and the child—mainly
because there is usually someone to work with at each lesson in
case of absences, and the child gains immeasurably from watching someone else in the same role. As the teacher gains experience she quickly comes to know who is capable of playing two
roles and how long it will take to rehearse and play certain
scenes. If there is an odd number, they may have to do an
extra scene or a single scene or playlet three times to accom-
modate the extra person. If possible, try to choose material
with fairly equal parts. This prevents jealousy.

Casting

Today we will read our scripts and completely cast everyone
if at all possible. Perhaps our teacher had no ideas of casting

in mind today. Perhaps she did. Or perhaps she intended only to read. With children of this age, she may have to rely on previous class experience, in addition to the readings, to help her cast her scenes effectively. Not all children with talent read well and expressively. Usually the two go hand in hand, but there are exceptions to the rule; and if a child has had good attendance all year and has done well with class assignments, then he deserves to be rewarded with a good role.

The teacher tries to read as many children in as many parts as she can before she casts the scene, and the lesson ends. If she cannot cast positively and finally today, she must do so at the next lesson, or there will be very little time left for rehearsal. If there are absentees and I know what parts they will play, I send them a copy of the script. (I always send absentees a copy of the lesson sheet so that they can come prepared next time.)

Today, boys and girls, I am not going to ask you to do anything but sit. Sit and read. Won't that be easy? Easy and fun! For I think reading is fun, don't you? And especially this kind of reading—play reading! Dialogue, which comes alive from the printed page, or script, after we give it meaning. These playlets and scenes which we will read today are the ones we will present for your parents and relatives at our last lesson. (*Squeals of delight and enthusiasm here.*)

I will call upon each of you to read one or more parts today. As you read I would like you to try to talk exactly as you think the character would, even though you have just been introduced to him. Read with your dress-up voice. Read with enthusiasm. Sit up and perk up. After we have read everything and everyone has read at least one part, I will tell you what role you are to play and give you the script to take home with you. Script is the actor's term for the copy of the scene or play that he uses for study. It comes from the Latin and means something written.

At the close of the reading the teacher tells each child what part he will play. She double checks to make sure he does not leave class without the correct script.

Be careful with your script. Take a colored pencil and underline your lines very carefully. Also underline the last few words of the speech ahead of yours. This is your *cue!* Study your part carefully. Start to learn your lines, and don't forget to bring a pencil when I see you next. Good-bye till then!

Lesson 25

1. Today we start work on our playlets or scenes.
2. These will be presented for parents and friends at the final lesson.
3. First we will read our material from start to finish so that you understand it completely.
4. Each of you will be called upon to read one or more parts.
5. Put forth a great deal of effort and read as well as you can.
6. In order to read well, you must use a good voice.
7. After you have all read one or more parts, your teacher will know what part you will be able to play best.
8. She will tell you what role you are to play.
9. She will give you a script.
10. Take good care of this script. You will bring it to class with you every lesson from now on.

Assignment for next lesson:

Be sure to bring your script and a pencil to class. Both are very important so don't forget them. We are going to block our playlet or scene. You already know what blocking means. Review in your mind stage directions. Study your part carefully and start to learn your lines. Take a colored pencil and underline your lines and cues. Do this neatly.

LESSON 26

Blocking and Script Marking

Today we clear up any casting problems we may have. Our teacher is certain that everyone in the class has at least one role before she begins one of the several duties she must check away during this lesson.

Reread to Understand Better

First we reread our scripts. At this reading, word pronunciation and meaning are clarified for the children. We also make sure that they understand their characters and each character's relation to the others in the play. We talk a little about plot, what the play is about.

Things to Do

We work quickly today. There is much to be done. Much of information about blocking that was related in Lesson 22 we repeat again at this lesson. The teacher sketches a ground plan of each playlet or scene and has each child do so on the back of his script. She blocks each scene with at least one cast. The other cast must observe carefully what its counterpart on stage is doing and mark its scripts accordingly. The teacher should supervise the marking of scripts and take the required time to see that this is being done correctly. In the case of some children this requires much supervision and patience, but it is better that we do it today; otherwise future lessons will be wasted on repetition.

Blocking

If time permits, have every child walk through the blocking today. Make sure that all turns, crosses, entrances, exits, all bits of business are carefully understood and executed the way the teacher wants them. We know that the children cannot work very freely with scripts in their hands, but if they start out with a fundamentally sound and simple blocking, rehearsals that are to follow will be more enjoyable. Our cornerstone is secure, and we can start building!

A Word to the Wise

If the teacher knows that she is not going to have elaborate settings, and the children ask (it is usually the older children) what kind of set they are going to have, the teacher should explain that the setting is going to be simple and *why*.

You know, boys and girls, that we have only eight lessons in which to prepare our scenes for presentation to your parents. Think what a little time that is. Only eight lessons! In school, if we met for eight days in a row, we would finish up in a week and a half, and you would have to work very fast, wouldn't you? This way, at least, you have time between lessons to absorb your blocking and learn your lines.

In our little playlets and scenes we are going to have very simple settings and costumes, because most of our attention during this whole production is going to be focused on you. You, the actors, are most important in our scenes.

With so little time left to us, wouldn't we be foolish to spend all of it worrying about costumes and scenery? Of course, I am going to let you wear costumes. You will be responsible for these yourselves, and we will talk more about them later. The setting will be very simple, mostly just furniture. But the most important thing in the whole production is *you*, the actor. We are most interested in seeing you and what you have learned, how you move, how you talk, how you listen, how you gesture, how you sit, how you stand. Are you relaxed? Do you seem to feel comfortable onstage? These are the things all of us who watch you will be interested in observing. So go home today and resolve to learn your lines, cues, and blocking perfectly for next lesson. Then we will get somewhere. After we have all of these problems out of the way, then we can start to act and this is the most fun of all—acting! This is what we have spent so many lessons preparing for. At last your chance has come. It is up to you.

Lesson 26

1. Today we are going to block our playlets or scenes.
2. Did you remember to bring your pencil? Remember, you must bring it every week from now on.
3. We learned how to block a scene several weeks ago. Remember?
4. Your teacher will give you directions, and you must write them on your script.
5. These directions will tell you where to go onstage as you play your part.
6. As you block your scene today, try to recall all the things that you have been taught so far regarding movement.
7. Remember to stand straight and tall.
8. Remember to start always on the upstage foot.
9. Try to think about the correct use of the upstage hand.
10. Start to consider how your character would walk, talk, and move.
11. Concentrate! Think today about what you are supposed to be doing.
12. Pay careful attention to your teacher, and be sure that you leave the class today with a thorough understanding of what you are to do in the play.

Assignment for next lesson:

Learn all lines for the next lesson and memorize the blocking. Only six lessons are left, and five of these must be used for rehearsal. Five hours is a very little time to rehearse, so have your lines and movement learned for next week in order that time will not be wasted. As you practice at home remember to memorize:

1. Lines
2. Blocking
3. Cues

LESSON 27

Lines and Cues

Before we can really sink our teeth into our acting project today and get deeply involved, there are always minor problems that have to be cleared away. If someone has missed the last two lessons, he will have missed the readings, casting, and blocking. Perhaps a few have missed the blocking only. Whatever the case, we will have to take time to catch him up so that he has somewhere to start.

Mechanics

If the teacher wishes, she may begin with a few line rehearsals. Simply have the children sit in their seats or on the stage and have them say their lines without looking at the script. If some do not know their lines, permit them to read from their script. Do not let them blunder through it without one. This wastes time and causes the other children to be very restless. Line rehearsals like this are good occasionally. They give the children a feeling of the overall unity and flow of the play.

We try to run through our playlets as often as possible, making certain that everyone becomes more familiar with the blocking as the lesson progresses. Today is a good day to try to time movement with lines. This is very difficult for most beginners. The teacher should not expect perfection. But she can impress them with its importance. Simple business, such as sewing or pouring tea, requires technique, too, and we talk about all these things today. Sitting down, standing up—and over and over again we reiterate, "Start moving with your upstage foot!" In the midst of all these mechanical things the teacher admonishes everyone to learn his lines to the letter so that all of our actors will learn the right cue.

A cue is very important. Like our friend the rabbit, the actor pricks up his ears when he hears the beginning familiar words of his cue. It is his signal to speak, sometimes also to rise, move, gesture, sit, or whatever you will. If the other actor is remiss on his cue, does not give it, or gives the wrong one instead, he can cause trouble. Lines are mixed up and switched; actors become nervous; and sometimes business and lines are repeated, things that were already done and said. So please learn your lines carefully—and pay particular attention to your *cue*. By the way, did you know that there is another word—queue? It is spelled differently but pronounced the same as cue—and one of its meanings is related to the theater. Everytime you stand in line waiting to get your ticket for the movies or theater, you are standing in a queue. How about that? Since it is time to go, I want to remind you again to learn all lines, cues, and blocking perfectly. We have only six lessons left to *act*.

Lesson 27

1. If you have been absent recently, be sure that you receive a script today and know what part you will play.
2. If not, make a firm attempt to do well with the line rehearsal.

3. Try to master today all the difficulties you meet in blocking.
4. Pay close attention to your movement.
5. Really try to incorporate your movement with the dialogue.
6. Start with the upstage foot. Remember your upstage hand.
7. Ask a question if there is something about the blocking you don't understand.

Assignment for next lesson:

Polish your blocking and business. Perfect lines and cues!

LESSON 28

Costumes and Props

Costumes

Somewhere in the early part of our last quarter the teacher must devote a certain amount of time to the explanation of costumes for our project. It might as well be now. The children are always quite excited about costuming, but it has to be handled carefully so that they don't get too involved with it to the exclusion of everything else. I try to keep it at a minimum. Sometimes this is difficult, especially when we have a few mothers around with the enthusiasm of a Cecil Beaton or a Coco Chanel. When we leave the costuming completely up to the child, it usually evolves that two or three characters look marvelous, while the rest of the cast has a kind of seedy neglectedness in comparison. If a teacher is dealing with any-

When we must use props that reveal important action in the play, then we must make sure that our audience sees and understands everything that we are doing.

where upward of thirty-eight to fifty children that day, it is impossible for her to take on the costumes as a personal project. So she leaves it up to the child—but with supervision. He is responsible for getting his own costume together.

Creating Our Own Costumes

If the children just play children in a modern setting, they may simply get a little more dressed up the day of the play (if the part calls for this). Boys wear long pants suits if playing adults. Girls, if they are playing adults, wear their mother's clothes and makeup. For a period costume the teacher may sketch something that she would like for the child, which he may take home to show his mother. Pictures will do here, too. Whatever trend she decides the costuming will take, the teacher must explain it to the children clearly and carefully so that they have an exact idea of what she wants, plus the time it will take to put it together. Then there should be periodic checkups to see how things are coming.

Just what is the teacher's approach to the costuming going to be? If she is too fastidious, she will soon notice her dissatisfaction lending an air of disenchantment to the rest of the group. Because it is impossible to be completely satisfied with everything the children contrive for their costumes, she must decide to overlook some of the concoctions and immaturities, even permit them. If she thumbs down everything, they will loose enthusiasm. I generally disapprove of things that are too distracting, too awkward for them to get around in, or just downright wrong for the character. Often the teacher will be pleasantly surprised at a child's ingenuity, and his mother's also. Pictures and sketches help the mother considerably.

Makeup

I generally let the children wear makeup, the girls, anyway —lipstick and rouge. This is kept at a minimum, and they can apply it at home. A dressing room will have to be available for those who have more than one role and need to change costumes. If our teacher has only one class to be concerned with, of course she may have them apply makeup in the dressing room under her supervision and take as long as they like. By this time she knows who will be the problem children and who will find costuming an easy matter. It should be a spontaneous thing. Let them think about their costumes for a while. We will discuss the costumes again at the dress rehearsal when we see them, and there will be time in the interim that follows to make any changes before the performance.

Props

We should start to work today with properties, or props. These may be stage props, which in our case are mostly very simple furniture; hand props, which the actor handles onstage, such as books, cups and saucers, teapots; and personal props, such as handkerchiefs, pipes, jewelry, or purses, sometimes a part of a costume.

Of course, the furniture we will be using in our scenes must be onstage today. If our lines are learned, as they should be, we must start working with hand and personal props, too. Only three rehearsal days are left. If someone is supposed to look at his pocket watch, he should have one with him (A toy watch will do.) and draw it from his pocket. If someone is supposed to twist her ring to make a little magic, she should wear a ring today so she can really twist it. These young actors must start working with their props today so that they can be completely at home with them on the day of the dress rehearsal.

Also try to impress upon them that actors look upon furniture with fondness. They are not afraid of it. It does not just decorate the stage. It is a help to the actor. He needs it. He handles it with care. He feels at home with it.

We hope that there was sufficient time today to run through the chosen plays, paying attention to lines and cues. With so many interruptions, we hope that we can cover all that.

Children, I hope that you will give a lot of thought to your costumes in the time that we have left. We want to make sure that our choice of costume is the best that we could possibly make. Look through your closets at home and see what you can come up with. Remember, too, to practice any bit of business that requires you to use dialogue and props. Doing this type of business well will show us what a good actor you have become.

Lesson 28

1. We must take several things into consideration today.
2. Your teacher will lead a discussion concerning costumes for our playlets.
3. Clear up all problems and questions at this lesson.
4. We will also run through all of our playlets and scenes, as scheduled.
5. We will work with all props that are necessary to the plays: stage, hand, and personal.
6. Polish all your business at this lesson.
7. Sharpen your cues and dialogue.

Assignment for next lesson:

Plan your costume at home. Continue to work on your lines and business. Start to think more about your character. What is he like, and how does he relate to the rest of the play?

LESSON 29

Character Development

Conversation About Character

After we all have assembled, the teacher asks, "What is a character?" Harry points at Paul and shouts, "He is! He is!" Everybody laughs, and there are more jokes about characters. Then we continue our discussion. Louise says that a character belongs to a person. It is part of his personality—what makes him good, what makes him bad.

Yes, you are right, Louise. This is one of the most significant meanings of the word—the moral qualities of a person, strongly developed and strikingly displayed. I think this is part of what we are after. Playwrights seek to draw people in their plays who have striking character traits. Think of those within the framework of your family and your friends. Many possess very strong character traits, don't they? Some are very loving, very gentle, while others are quickly angered or cruel or cunning. Do you have friends who are intensely loyal? If you do, you are very lucky.

Man is represented or symbolized or portrayed as a character by the playwright who writes the play. He gives character to, or characterizes, the people that he writes about. He describes their individual qualities.

Now above and beyond what we see in the script about the character is what the actor sees in him. The actor must lend to this character, who is only written on paper, something of his own personality as well. The actor uses his mind, his imagination,

The three boys in the foreground of this picture are learning to shift their attention and concentration to where the action is, thus emphasizing the important focal point of the scene.

and his body to create this character, to make him come alive. This is called *characterization,* and how well he does this depends upon a number of attributes, or qualities, that the actor has bottled up inside him. What do you think some of these qualities might be? Let's think of a few, shall we? Ken?

"Let me see. Something the actor has bottled up inside of him. Hmm. Blood!"

Everybody laughs again. We are in a mood for laughter today.

"Now, Ken, this isn't a science class. We are studying drama today. But if you didn't have any blood, you wouldn't be able to feel, would you? You would be a corpse. So we can put that down as first on the list, can't we? The actor must have feeling. Another word for this is emotion. He must have emotion. He needs to have emotion when he attempts characterization."

"Now, something else. If you are playing an old person, someone much older than yourself, what are you going to use to help you play the character? After all, you are not very old. What will you do about it? Ellen?"

"My grandmother!" This from Doris.

"Right, Doris. Your experience with your grandmother will be a great help. But maybe your grandmother is kind most of the time, and this old lady is crotchety and bad-tempered. What will you do about it? Ellen?"

"I'll just think of Miss Frank, a cranky old maid down the street. Everytime a crowd of us roller-skate, she calls the police."

Ron intervenes. "I'll just think of my grandmother everytime she gets tired baby-sitting. Boy, is she crotchety!"

What Doris and Ellen and Ron have just told us implies that they have been using *observation* to help them with characterization. Older and experienced actors study their parts deeply and meaningfully to grasp the traits that lie within their characters.

They study the background, life, and writings of the playwright very intently for more clues. Also, the added experience of just living has taught them a lot—made them better actors. These are things you children cannot always do. But you can search within the lines of your character for special words that tell you more about him. Sometimes the playwright has another character throw more light on the subject. Then we start to add certain little touches to our character. If we happen to be playing the part of Jack in *Jack and the Beanstalk*, we discover that Jack is happy, kind, friendly, and lazy, don't we? What might he do to show us these qualities? (*Answers here:* "Smile," "Help people," "Be kind," "Yawn," etc.) Of course, the actor has to find the proper place in the script to show these traits. In *Little Women* we know that Beth is shy; Meg is ladylike and motherly; Jo is a tomboy; and Amy is proud and vain. Think of ways each actress could show us these qualities. (*We discuss.*)

This is an attempt at a more or less superficial search for characterization, but only certain children have the understanding to probe deeper. This experimentation helps them to understand what characterization really is, what we are after. We hope they will find the characteristics and impressions that are already there in the script. If a part seems to lack definition and character, the teacher can always add significant business for the actors who seem to need it. The important point is that the children should grasp the essence of the character, and it should shine through their playing. If a vocal characterization helps them to achieve this goal, let them do it!

Lesson 29

1. Before we start rehearsal today, we will have a discussion of characterization.
2. CHARACTER is the term given to every person who is written into the play by the playwright.
3. We know this word, character, has several other meanings.

4. It also applies to the moral qualities of a person that make up his personality.
5. The actor must lend his personality to his character and add dimension to the role that he is playing.
6. He does this with the use of his mind, body, will, and imagination.
7. He brings feeling and observation to the character.
8. Think of those around you who have strong character traits. What are they?

Assignment for next lesson:

Our performance day is fast approaching. Only two rehearsal days are left. Practice your parts carefully at home and continue to develop your character. To help yourself more, list the traits you know your character to possess and see if you are able to convey this to your audience.

LESSON 30

Imagination and Character

In the line rehearsals that the teacher holds occasionally the children sense the flow or unity of the scene or playlet. When we have run-through rehearsals often, they begin to sense the plot development. This awareness is very important to their total feeling of accomplishment. Run-through rehearsals (rehearsals without stops) should take place often from the beginning. They give the children the feeling that we really rehearsed today. "We did our scene!" "We did our play!" It is easy enough to get started and then get all crossed up with that scene with Molly and Don because it is one of the better scenes or they need extra help. Of course, some scenes will require extra work, and the teacher will have to set a part of each period aside for this. But everyone should have at least one run-through of his scene at every rehearsal. Make it an absolute must to try to cover everyone at every rehearsal. Run-through rehearsals give the child the beginnings of a sense of timing, a sense of immediacy, and a sense of urgency, so important to every actor. The play becomes more important; there is more excitement about getting it done.

The Finer Points

Then, too, as we rehearse today let us sharpen our sensitivity and the finer points of our imaginations.

1. As we await the entrance of someone whom we expect, can we feel excitement in the air?
2. Can we almost hear someone else at the other end of the line in that telephone conversation?
3. When Jane says, "This cocoa is delicious," do our mouths water, too.
4. Can we smell the perfume of those roses?
5. Are we really shivering in this terrible cold?
6. Do we think we will faint in this terrific heat?

Try to get the children to look directly at the other people in the scene. This will help their concentration.

Dos and Don'ts

Unless the part calls for it, which it rarely does, the girls should not be permitted to wear pants and heavy boots to rehearsals. If they have to tumble on the floor or faint, I permit pants for a while until they have mastered their business. It is

This boy and girl are only a few years apart in age, but it is our imagination that helps to convince us that she is the mother and he is her son.

very difficult to get decidedly feminine movement from girls in pants. They simply get too relaxed.

The teacher discovers that she will have to correct foot positions a great deal with most of the children in this age group. In sitting and standing positions they do awkward things with their hands and feet. When a child reveals extreme sensitivity to movement and is very conscious of these elements after they have been pointed out to him, usually we should be aware of his special talent. This is a sign of a natural actor: careful, economical movement, intelligent, expressive line readings—qualities that subtly and delightfully make us aware and sit up and take notice. We know that we are in the presence of talent. This is a pleasurable and exciting discovery.

Lesson 30

1. Today we will run through our scenes and playlets as often as time will permit.
2. Think about your characterization. Try all the things that you have been thinking about.
3. Use your imagination for everything: seeing, smelling, tasting, feeling, and hearing.
4. Be graceful. Move easily. Sit and stand comfortably.
5. Look at and listen to the other actors. Players must play together.
6. That is what you are—players, another word for actors.

Assignment for next lesson:

Our next lesson is the dress rehearsal. Be on time next week with all costumes and props. We will begin promptly. Remember, check everything carefully before you leave home.

LESSON 31

Dress Rehearsal

We treat our dress rehearsal today much the same as we did in Lesson 15. The teacher gets as accurate a number as possible of those relatives and friends who are coming to the actual performance. We assume that she has been working with lights and curtain all along. If the children are going to pull the curtain, they need constant practice with this.

Final Points

If they have not done so before, they should rehearse their bows today. Close the curtain at the ending of the scene or playlet. This may be a slow or fast curtain, as the teacher wishes. Have the cast assemble in appropriate places on a straight line within the boundary of the curtain. Someone in the middle of the line should gently incline his head forward, starting the bow. Arms and hands are kept at the sides. The bow is executed slowly, from the waist down. The head is up, with the actor smiling at the audience. As the bow is finished, the curtain closes again. If she wants another bow, the teacher should notify the cast.

Check makeup, costumes, and all props before the rehearsal starts today. Make sure there is a table in a convenient place for hand props and that all the children know where it is. Excitement runs high these last few days. Many of the children are jittery and nervous. Mistakes that occur because of nervousness are unavoidable and sad. Children who have done beautifully all through the rehearsal period can easily crack up over a very small thing. Try to keep them relaxed and calm, and make sure there are no surprises in the technical development of things.

By this time the teacher surely knows who is going to announce the program. Will she do it, or will the children do it? In classes with eight-, nine-, and ten-year-olds the teacher will feel that it is best if she announces the program. Many times I permit the eleven- and twelve-year-olds to announce it themselves, especially those who have smaller roles in the scenes. If the teacher wishes a printed program, fine! This saves time and explanation.

At last all of our technical problems seem to be taken care of.

Now are we ready to begin? Isn't it exciting and breathtaking? Everything that we have been rehearsing, creating, imagining, working for has reached its time of fulfillment. We are just about to hatch our theatrical eggs. Right? Of course, we are missing one very important element today, the audience. But they will be here soon again, and we will be even better at that time, won't we? We are fortunate to have this opportunity to prepare for them. As you go through your scene or playlet today, remember always to play as you would for an audience; for after all, that is whom you want to communicate with, show yourselves to, is it not? When we act for an audience we are telling them, "Watch us closely now. We are going to tell you a story with words and movement. See? This is how it is." Be charming, enjoyable, and entertaining. At last you are actors!

Lesson 31

1. Today is our dress rehearsal.
2. This is our final chance to iron out wrinkles and mistakes.
3. Be sure that your teacher approves of your costume and makeup.
4. Check all types of props that are necessary for your role.
5. Try to keep calm and relaxed.

6. Tell your teacher the number of relatives and friends you are bringing to the performance.
7. Make sure you understand how to bow correctly.
8. Be sure that you know when your scene occurs on the program.

Assignment for next lesson:

Our next lesson is our most important day. We perform for an audience. We have been working toward this day for a long time. In the time that remains, work hard on your character. Don't forget your costumes and props. Above all, don't forget your parents.

LESSON 32

Performance

Actors, Adieu!

Today is our final lesson, our performance day. It is "hello day" to some parents we haven't met, and "good-bye day" to the children—at least for a while. We prepare for this day very much as we did for the presentation of the record pantomime in Lesson 16.

After everyone is seated, the teacher begins to speak:

We are very happy indeed to have such a wonderful audience for our playlets and scenes today. I think those of you who came to see us at the end of the second quarter understand just what it is we are doing in this class. This is a beginner's class in acting. We are presenting today an acting project on which we have been working for the past seven weeks.

Why are the children doing this? Well, because, being children, they wish to act, to imitate, to recreate life. They enjoy painting, too, and coloring, which are means of portraying also—aren't they? They have a drive to perform, carry out, project. They wish to show you, the audience, the most important elements of our plot today.

We are so anxious to have you empathize with us, as we represent in mimic action an ideal or incident or story. And when we toss our crystal balloon of words and thoughts and feelings across the footlights to you, will you not gently, silently, tap it and send it back to us. But hush! Our actors are ready. Can't you sense the excitement in their quiet breathing? They are ready to wield a certain kind of magic.

Places, everybody. Houselights out. *Curtain!*

Lesson 32

1. At last it is the day for our performance.
2. Actors are usually very nervous at times like this, but relax; breathe deeply; and try to be calm.
3. Sit quietly in your seat until it is time for you to go onstage.
4. As you start to act with your partners onstage, look at them; listen to them; and concentrate.
5. Good Luck!!
6. Have fun!
7. Enjoy the magic of playing.

Assignment for next lesson:

Alas! There is none. I shall miss you very much, but I know that we will see one another again soon.

Playlets for Study

Coffee

CHARACTERS
CATHY
ALICE

SCENE: *A living room. Doorbell rings.* CATHY *enters in dress-up clothes from door Right Stage. Crosses room to door Left. Admits* ALICE, *who is carrying a suitcase.*

CATHY: You're late. I thought you'd never get here.

ALICE: We got stuck in traffic. There was a wreck on the parkway. A big smashup.

CATHY: Gee! Anybody killed?

ALICE: I don't know. I didn't see any bodies. I guess the ambulance came and went by the time we passed it.

CATHY: Well, come on. Let's get started. No one's here. We can have the living room.

ALICE: Great! What'll we play?

CATHY: Let's play Coffee. Hurry up and get dressed. I've got the coffee all made.

ALICE: Ugh! I hate it. I'll never get used to drinking it.

CATHY: I know, but they all drink it. My mother had a Coffee in here the other morning, and one woman drank eight cups.

ALICE: No kiddin'. She must have a percolator for a stomach.

CATHY: Well, let's get going. How do you like my shoes?

ALICE: Neat! (*She opens suitcase. Takes out clothes.*) They your mom's? (*Starts to get dressed.*)

CATHY: Yes. She just got them. I'd get killed if she knew I was wearing them now.

ALICE: (*Throws dress over herself. Puts on beads.*) I borrowed Clare's new lipstick. Want to try it? (*Hands it to* CATHY.)

CATHY: Oh, what a devastating shade. Red Ebony. (*Starts to put it on.*)

ALICE: It looks terrific on. Here, give it to me. I have to be sure it's back on her dresser before she gets home. (*She takes it. Smears it on quickly. Puts on a hat.*) Well, I'm ready. Let's go.

CATHY: Okay. Let's start where you come in. Go on outside.

ALICE: All right, but don't keep me waiting. It's cold out there. (*She goes outside.* CATHY *exits door Right. Doorbell rings.*)

CATHY: (*Crosses room. Opens door Left.*) Irma, dar-r-r-ling! It's so good to see you.

ALICE (*kissing her*): Oh, Ida. I'm so glad to be here. Long time no see. (*She giggles.*)

CATHY: Now take off your hat and be comfortable. What a beautiful chapeau! So chic!

ALICE: Do you like it? I thought it was so pretty, too. Got it at the Juliette Shop.

CATHY: Why, it's simply cunning. Now come and sit down and tell me all the news. I'm just dying to find out what's new with you. (*She leads* ALICE *over to the sofa, Right Center, in front of which is a coffee table.*) Now sit down and get comfy while I get some coffee for us.

ALICE: Oh good, it's time for my coffee break.

CATHY: Now just get relaxed and I'll be right back. (*Exits Right.* ALICE *smoothes her hair. Primps a little. Looks around the room.*)

CATHY: (*Returns with coffee and things. Places them on table.*) Here we are (*gaily laughing*).

ALICE: Don't they look delicious! But I don't dare take one, you know. I have to count my calories.

CATHY: Well, darling, you don't have to worry about these. They're noncaloric. I get them at a dear little bakery store around the corner—Rumplemayer's. He makes them just for a group of us calorie-conscious women in the neighborhood.

ALICE: In that case, Irma dear, I'll try one. Just a nibble. (*She tastes one.*) Hmm. This is really good!

CATHY: Cream?

ALICE: No thank you, dear.

CATHY: Sugar?

ALICE: No dear. Just black. Nice and strong and black. (CATHY *sits and pours. Hands her coffee. She takes a cup.*)

CATHY: Now, tell me. What's this I hear about June and Edna? Florence tells me they are going back to work.

ALICE: Yes, Irma. June is going to open a knitting shop on Oliver Avenue, and Edna started back to teaching in September.

CATHY: Isn't that something! Sometimes I think of doing such things. I'm in such a rut, you know.

ALICE: You, Irma? I can't believe it! With your Symphony, and the Garden Club, and the Thursday Musical Club. I don't see how you could ever be bored.

CATHY: I know, dear, but I was just saying to Harold the other evening, "If only I could do something different. Life is so dull."

ALICE: That's just the way I feel at times. Bridge, bridge, bridge— and golf, golf, golf! Really, it drives me to distraction. (*Phone rings.*)

CATHY: Excuse me, Ida. (*Answers phone.*) Warner's residence. Yes. Yes, I will. Right away. Okay. Bye. (*Turns to* ALICE.) Yipes! It was Mom. She's on her way home and wants me to light the oven for dinner. She said we can make Brownies.

ALICE: Yippee! Hurray! I'm just in the mood for Brownies. I wasn't in the mood for coffee.

CATHY: Well, hurry up! Let's get this junk off! My feet are killing me! (*They quickly undress. There is disarray everywhere.*)

CATHY: You can crack the nuts while I sift the flour.

ALICE: Okay? Race you? Last one in the kitchen's a green onion. (*They exit together Right.*)

Curtain

Dreamdust for Shadows

CHARACTERS

DREAM MAKER (*maker of dreams*)
DUSTY (*his assistant*)
GIRL SHADOW
BOY SHADOW

SCENE: *The* DREAM MAKER'S *workshop, where he manufactures dreams. Everything imaginable is here—balloons, stars, moons, masks, monsters, animals, pillows—everything you find in dreams. The* DREAM MAKER *is at Right Stage sitting at his desk. On the desk is a large, unusual caldron from which he takes large, colorful stars one at a time. He writes something on each one, then stamps it with a stamper. As he finishes stamping,* DUSTY, *his assistant, comes and gets each star and hangs it on a clothesline affair. They are very businesslike about all this. All of a sudden we hear the sound of a whistle. They both look up.*

DREAM M: Aha, there goes the silver whistle.

DUSTY: It's a girl this time. I can always tell. Boys blow the blue horn, but girls always blow the silver whistle.

DREAM M: Blue is for boys, you know, Dusty. Down on earth when a baby is born—if it's a boy, they shower it with blue presents. If it's a girl, then the presents are pink. That is, if the baby is lucky and receives many gifts. (*Now we hear the sound of a horn blowing.*)

DUSTY: There it goes. Now someone is blowing the horn. It's a boy. I know it. There must be two out there—a boy and a girl.

DREAM M: That's unusual. It's been a long time since a boy and a girl visited us together. Who can it be?

DUSTY: The wind is disturbed about it, too. Just listen to him howl.

DREAM M: Oh, that's just impatience. He's always impatient in February. Can't wait for it to be March. That's his month. Hurry, and let them in. (DUSTY *crosses to door Left. With great ceremony, lifts the latch. A shivering* BOY *and* GIRL *enter. The* BOY *wears a tassel cap. The* GIRL *wears a long, colorful scarf, twirled around her neck and head.*)

GIRL: Oh, but it is cold out there.

BOY: (*Puts hands to ears.*) Oh, my ears, my ears! Are they still there? Do I have ears?

GIRL: (*Puts hands to nose.*) Oh, my nose, my nose! Is it still there? Do I have a nose?

DUSTY: (*Goes to* BOY. *Feels ears.*) Yes, you have ears. They are still there. (*Crosses to* GIRL. *Feels nose.*) And you have a nose. It is still there.

BOY AND GIRL TOGETHER: Oh, good! Good! We are so glad that they are still there!

DREAM M: Who are you? Dreamers?

BOY: We really do not know who we are.

GIRL: What are dreamers?

DUSTY: Dreamers are boys and girls who come here to the Dream Maker. They want his dreams.

GIRL: (*To* DREAM MAKER.) Are you the Dream Maker?

DREAM M: Yes, I am the Dream Maker. This is my shop. My workshop. (*He gestures with a wave of his hand.*) And this is the stuff that dreams are made of. (*Pointing around.*)

BOY (*looking at room*): How interesting!

GIRL (*looking at stars and moons*): How mysterious!

BOY (*examining stars*): How beautiful!

GIRL (*looking at masks and monsters*): How ugly!

BOY (*with arms outflung*): How incomprehensible!

GIRL: How cozy! (*She is comfortable and warm.*)

DREAM M: True! True! How true! I like the words you use. They truly apply to my shop. Interesting. Beautiful. Incomprehensible. Ugly. Yes! Yes! Mysterious. Beautiful. Yes! Yes! (*He is pleased and excited.*) Come and sit down. Be comfortable. Dusty, fetch them some brew. (*They sit on a bench Down Left.* DUSTY *crosses Upstage Right. Takes teapot. Pours into two small cups. Brings it to visitors.*)

GIRL: (*Sips brew.*) Delicious!

(DREAM MAKER *pulls chair from desk to Down Left. Sits.* DUSTY *sits on a stool Downstage Center.*)

DUSTY: You say you do not know who you are? Are you not dreamers? Only dreamers come here to the Dream Maker.

GIRL: We really do not know who we are, but we have been told that we are shadows.

DUSTY: Who told you that?

GIRL: Children!

DREAM M: Children! So you have been with the children, have you?

BOY: Yes. The children have told us that we are shadows.

GIRL: But only when they got angry with us or impatient.

BOY: When we couldn't shout back at them.

GIRL: Or smell the flowers they picked.

BOY: Or catch the balls they threw.

GIRL: Or tie their shoes or their sashes for them.

DREAM M: I see. I see. That is understandable. Children are very impatient. But it is strange that you did not know that you were shadows. Very strange.

GIRL: But you see, we do not look like shadows.

DUSTY: Not in those impossible clothes! Where did you get that tassel cap—and that ridiculous scarf?

GIRL: I only remember jumping out of a trunk with this—ridiculous scarf, as you call it—tied tightly around my ears and neck.

BOY: And I once was a snowman who melted—and was left only with this impossible cap hugging my head.

DREAM M: Then you didn't come together?

DUSTY: Where did you meet?

GIRL: We met one evening at day's end in a garden underneath a birdbath with a sundial on it—just as the sun was sinking, all aglow, into her bed of purple and red and gold, exactly at that moment when shadows disappear over the edge of the earth . . .

BOY: . . . and scramble into that mountain of gray and black they call the Palace of Darkness. But the gates of the drawbridge that led us to the castle had already closed.

GIRL: And there we were. Left in the middle of nowhere. Too late for twilight . . .

BOY: . . . and too early for midnight.

GIRL: And we've been wandering around like this ever since.

BOY: Until we saw your sign. The sign that said, "This way to the Dream Maker, the Maker of Dreams. Here lies the stuff that dreams are made of."

GIRL: We thought that perhaps you could make us look more like shadows.

BOY: Can you help us, even if we are not dreamers?

DREAM M: Well, I'm not so sure that you are not dreamers. It seems to me that you might be harboring a little dream there. Wouldn't you say so, Dusty?

DUSTY: Yes, sir. I would say so, sir. A little longing—a little hankering after something—a thought—a wish—a desire. That's all you need to have a dream.

DREAM M: Let's take a look in our costume box and see what we can rig up for you. What colors would you like?

GIRL: Oh, purple. Purple, of course. The most beautiful shadows wear purple.

BOY: Not for me. No siree. I prefer black or gray or both. They are more majestic. Kings are cloaked in black or gray.

GIRL: Purple is the robe of queens!

DREAM M: Well, no matter. See what you can find, Dusty.

DUSTY (*digging through costume box*): We have many robes here, and capes and capelets and cloaks. Ah, here is something. (*Drags out a cloak affair with a hood.*)

GIRL: (*Grabs it.*) Oh, perfect! Perfect! Just what I was hoping for. (*She tries it on. Primps in it.*) I am beautiful now.

BOY (*disappointed*): Have you something for me? Oh, I hope you have something for me.

DUSTY: Have patience now. I'm coming to the bottom of the box. You are as bad as the children. No patience. Ah, here is something that I think you'll like. (*Holds up black and gray cape with hood.*)

Boy: At last. Oh, wonderful. Yes. Yes. That is exactly what I need. (*Puts it on.*) Now I am truly a shadow. The hood is perfect! (*Prances around in it.*)

Dream M: Well, I'm relieved that you are satisfied. We can usually find just the right thing for you here. Now, would you like to to take one of my pillows and have a little dream before you leave?

Boy: Oh, no, we must be off. We want to reach dawn before day.

Girl: And day before dusk!

Dream M: Come, come now. I don't see the necessity for all this rush! Just when we were getting acquainted. Come, won't you have a little more of my brew?

Dusty: Before we say adieu!

Girl: Oh, no. We must leave! I suppose you'll think us truly ill-mannered, rushing off so, but we are so terribly anxious to try our new costumes. And dawn is approaching. We hope you'll understand.

Boy: (*Takes a large watch and chain from a hook.*) By the way, Dream Maker, do you think I might have this ornament to wear around my neck. It will dress me up, don't you think—and besides, I would like to have a souvenir.

Dream M: Certainly, certainly. A timepiece is an invaluable aid to a shadow. It will help you to be on time for that appointment with the drawbridge.

Girl: And Dream Maker, would you mind terribly if I took this trinket. (*She lifts key on chain from another hook.*) It looks so ornamental—and practical.

Dream M: Quite right, my dear. Yes, you may certainly have it. Not only will it serve as a personal souvenir from me, but it will also be an indispensable aid just in case you are late at the gate of the drawbridge. Did you notice if the gate had a keyhole?

Girl: Yes, there is a hole in the gate. Right in the middle. But I did not know what it was for. A keyhole! How precious! And now I have a key to go with it. Just think of the things I shall be able to do!

DUSTY: Isn't that just like a girl?

BOY: If that key will really fit the drawbridge, that means we can enter the Shadow Palace whenever we like.

DREAM M: Oh, it will fit. It will fit. Never fear. I have keys to fit all locks and dreams to suit all dreamers.

DUSTY: And timepieces recording the time in Dreamland, Nomansland, Wonderland, and Shadowland. I personally set these timepieces myself. It is curious, isn't it, Dream Maker, that the boy shadow has chosen the Shadowland timepiece without knowing it?

BOY: Have I? How clever of me!

GIRL: Goodness!

DREAM M: Yes, it is curious. Curious, and quite a coincidence. Really it is. I have been looking for someone to help me with the tardy shadows in Shadowland. Some of them are very tardy, you know. When the children come to get their dreams from me, they are sometimes late, and we have a great lineup waiting patiently for their dreams. They tell me this is the fault of the shadows, who are sometimes very tardy about going back to Shadowland at dusk and linger around the rooms where the children sleep. This keeps the children awake and they can't get started for Dreamland on time. I desperately need a timekeeper and gatekeeper in Shadowland. Someone to make sure that the shadows know it is time to come back to the Palace of Darkness, and someone to see that the gate doesn't close until they are all in.

DUSTY: I think you have found the right helpers, Dream Maker. Here they are.

DREAM M: Would you like to help me?

GIRL: Oh, yes. Yes. It sounds exciting!

BOY: Think how important we will be.

DREAM M: At last my problem has been solved. Now wrap your cloaks tightly around you. Sprinkle them with Dreamdust, Dusty. (*He does so.*) (*To* BOY.) Be sure to set the alarm at dusk every evening. (*To* GIRL.) And be sure to stay at the gates to see that they are all in. In a short time I will send Dusty down to see how you are getting along. Good luck, now. And be good shadows!

BOY AND GIRL: Good-bye! Good-bye, Dream Maker! And thank you! We will. Good-bye. (*They exit.*)

DUSTY: (*Bars door.*) Well, sir. That was a stroke of luck. I hope they can do the job for you, sir.

DREAM M: I hope so, Dusty. Responsibility will be good for them, for I believe they are the tardy little shadows the children have been complaining about. If they have something to keep them busy, they'll stay out of mischief, I'm sure.

DUSTY: Yes, sir. Everyone should shoulder some sort of responsibility. Now the children will arrive on time for their dreams.

DREAM M: And we can manufacture bigger and better and more entertaining dreams for all children everywhere. Right, Dusty?

DUSTY: Right you are, sir. (*He salutes.*)

Curtain

The Secret of the Old Cave

CHARACTERS
HANK
RICH

SCENE: *An old cave. Two boys enter with flashlights. One is carrying a map. They shine their lights around.*

RICH (*flashing light over walls*): Well, this is the last cave on the list, isn't it? It better be, or I quit. (*He sits.*)

HANK (*with light and map, searching around walls*): It is. Hallelujah! It is! Look over here. Hurry up! Here are the three *x*'s.

RICH: (*Rises. Crosses Right.*) Well, I'll be a monkey's uncle. I never thought we'd find it. You're right, for sure. These are the three *x*'s. What do you know? I never thought I'd live to see the day when I, personally, Richard Warren Hillsdale, would be the discoverer of the secret of the old cave!

HANK: Ahem! Codiscoverer! And you know *who*, personally, put most of the work into this little project. But let's not quibble over such minor details. This is the most exciting day of our lives, don't forget. Let's get on with the discovery.

RICH: Are you really sure this is it? Positive?

HANK: (*Hands him the map.*) Here. Look for yourself. There's no mistaking it. These are the three *x*'s. Etched into the wall. And this cave is grayer than the others. Scott told me that's what the original map said. That this cave is gray and chalky-looking, while the others in this area are black.

RICH: Well, so far, so good. Now what else do we look for? What are we supposed to find here? Silver? Gold? Buried treasure? A Spanish chest? What?

HANK: Who knows? The cave has a secret. Right?

RICH: If you say so. You've lived in Frostburg longer than I have. Who told you about it?

HANK: Well, when I first moved here three years ago, the other kids were always talking about the caves in the hills—that there were a lot of them, you know—and every now and then we'd go on a hike and explore one. But I never did actually hear about this cave with the secret until just this past summer. Scott told me. He knows all about it. He even gave me this map.

RICH: How did he find out about it?

HANK: Oh, he's lived here all his life. His dad and his uncles grew up here, too. They've heard about it for centuries.

RICH: Centuries!

HANK: Yes siree! Centuries! Whatever this secret is, man, it's old!

RICH (*impressed*): Boy!! Well, we better get started looking around to see if we can unearth something. Wow! This place sure smells!

HANK (*superior*): Naturally. We're probably the first ones to enter here in eons.

RICH: No kidding? Well, I guess that's right. Hey, what's this over here? (*He kicks something out of the floor of the cave.*) A shoe? a tennis shoe! It's old, but—say—they didn't wear tennis shoes centuries ago, did they?

HANK: No, of course not. Let me see. Yes, it's a tennis shoe, all right. (*He is baffled. Mood changes.*) Ssh! Quiet! Listen! Do you hear anything?

RICH: No. Nothing.

HANK: Well, somebody's been here. That's for sure. I wonder if they found anything. I mean, the secret.

RICH: Maybe there is no secret. What else does the map say? (*Looks at map.*) What's that circle?

HANK: I don't know what it means. It's in the cave, though. The only thing I see here is this rock.

RICH: Maybe the rock has something to do with the secret. That's probably what the circle means. The rock!

HANK: It must! Let's try to move it! (*They push the rock.*)

RICH: Gosh! It's heavy, but it's moving. (*Finally it gives.*) There! Hey! Here's a hole! And something's in it! (*They dig a little with searchlights and fingers.*) It's a box! A tin box!

HANK: With the secret! The secret! (*He is terribly excited.*) The secret's in it. Hooray! We've found it. The secret of the old cave!! At last, after all this searching. Here, give it to me. Hurry up! Hurry up! (*Grabs box.*)

RICH: Calm down! Calm down! Take it easy.

HANK: Look. There's a note inside! I—I can't read it very well. (*Hands it to* RICH.) Here. You read it. I'm too excited. Hurry up! Hurry up! What does it say?

RICH: Hold on, will you? I'm trying to figure it out. The guy who wrote this can't even print.

HANK (*very impatient*): Come on.

RICH (*slowly*): "The person who discovers the secret of the old cave is a GREAT BIG GOON—Ha ha ha. This is IT—Ha ha ha ha." Well, I'll be . . .

HANK (*wildly excited*): I'll get him! I'll get him! I'll get him for this. That Scott! Just wait till I get my hands on him. Just wait! Just wait! (*He exits Upstage Left.*)

RICH: Hey, wait! Wait for me. Remember, I don't know how to get out of this place. Hey, Hank, wait for me! Secret caves! Treasure lore! Bah! Humbug!

Curtain

Another Day

CHARACTERS

MOTHER
FATHER
SANDY
BYRON
AGNES (*the maid*)

SCENE: *A pleasant, sunny dining room. It is breakfast time.* MOTHER *is at the table reading the morning paper and sipping coffee. The phone rings. The* MAID *enters from the kitchen and answers it.*

AGNES: Andrews' residence. Who? Gus? No. No. You have the wrong number. We have no one here by that name.

MOTHER (*looking up from paper*): Who was that, Agnes?

AGNES: Wrong number, Mrs. Andrews. Someone wanted Gus.

MOTHER: That's funny. Someone called yesterday asking for Gus.

AGNES: (*Looks up as she clears some dishes away from table.*) I knew a Gus once. Gus Mushrush. Used to go with my sister Grace.

MOTHER: What an unusual name!

FATHER: (*Enters. Kisses* MOTHER. *Sits at other end of table.*) Good morning, dear. Morning, Agnes.

AGNES (*standing at the table*): Good morning, Mr. Andrews. Going to have the usual this morning?

FATHER: Got any oatmeal out there, Agnes?

AGNES (*without much enthusiasm*): Yes, sir.

FATHER: I feel like a bowl of good, hot oatmeal this morning. Something that'll stick to my ribs.

AGNES (*resigned expression on her face*): Is that all, sir?

FATHER: Oh-h-h-h—I think I'll have some juice, two soft-boiled eggs, some toast, and coffee. Got that, Agnes?

AGNES (*woeful expression as she memorizes menu*): Yes, sir. (*Exits.*)

MOTHER: I think you really surprised Agnes with that menu just now, Arnold. She was only prepared for the usual toast and coffee.

FATHER: Threw a curve, did I? Well, every now and then it's good to throw a few curves. Shakes things up a bit.

MOTHER: I know, dear, but Agnes is used to a routine. She needs a little preparation for surprises. I hope it didn't upset her too much.

FATHER: Doris, are you trying to tell me that Agnes has to be handled with kid gloves. (*raising his voice*) Thundering Thor, she's costing me enough!

MOTHER: Sssh! Arnold! She'll hear you.

SANDY (*entering*): Morning, Mother. Morning, Dad. Isn't it gorgeous this morning?

FATHER (*moodily*): What's gorgeous about it?

SANDY (*ecstatically*): Oh, just everything! The sky! The trees! The leaves! It's all so beautiful. Fall is my favorite season. (*Starts humming.*) I've got to call Cindy.

AGNES: (*Enters with juice. Places it at* FATHER's *place.*) Having your usual, Miss Sandy?

SANDY: Yes, Agnes, but instead of toast, I think I'll have a toasted English muffin with cinnamon apple jelly. Not too dark please.

AGNES (*stiffening up*): Sorry. No English muffins, and we only got marmalade.

SANDY: Oh, all right. Toast and marmalade. And it *was* such a beautiful morning. . . .

AGNES: (*Exits muttering.*) Toasted English muffin! You'd think it was Howard Johnson's.

SANDY (*at phone Left of Upstage Center entrance, dialing*): Hello, Cindy—Sandy. No. Just wondered what you're wearing. The red and white. Okay. Then I'll wear my blue and pink. Okay. See you later. (*Hangs up.*)

MOTHER: What was that all about?

SANDY: Oh, nothing much. We sit next to each other in study hall, and just didn't want to clash, that's all.

FATHER: That would really be a disaster, wouldn't it, daughter?

SANDY: Now, Popsy. (*Crosses to him. Hugs him.*) You know I could use a couple of dollars. I need them really bad.

FATHER: Popsy will get you nowhere.

SANDY: Ah, come on. Please, Dad. We've really had a lot of expenses this week.

FATHER: Talk it over with your mother. She handles the budget.

MOTHER: Really, Sandy, I think you're overspent.

SANDY: A lot of unexpected things have come up, Mom. You wouldn't dream!

(AGNES *enters with food for* SANDY *and* FATHER. *Byron enters Upstage Center.*)

BYRON: Good morning, all. What's for breakfast, Aggie?

MOTHER: I told you not to call Agnes Aggie, Byron.

AGNES (*firmly*): The usual breakfast we always have.

BYRON: You know what, Aggie—er—Agnes, how would you feel like shaking everything up this morning and having some pancakes and sausages for a change?

AGNES: That would take entirely too long, Byron. Sausages take quite awhile to cook.

BYRON: (*Crosses to* AGNES.) Ah, come on, Agnes. You're the best cook in the city; you know it!

AGNES (*beginning to melt. He is clearly her favorite*): Well (*smiling a little*) if you don't mind waiting. (*Exits.*) (BYRON *sits.*)

SANDY: Boy, do you rate! (*Phone rings. She answers it.*) Hello. Who? Gus? No. You have the wrong number.

BYRON: Hey, wait a minute. That's for me. (*Grabs phone.*) Hi! Sure. Fine. I'll meet you in the locker room. So long.

FATHER: Since when are people calling you Gus?

BYRON: Since Monday, Dad. It's my new and permanent nickname.

FATHER: Gus!

MOTHER: Gus!

SANDY: Gus! Disgusting!

MOTHER: Oh, Byron. Why?

BYRON: Well, what did you expect? Giving me a name like Byron. You didn't expect me to keep it when I got old enough to have any sense, did you?

FATHER: And so you came of age on Monday, did you? I see nothing wrong with the name Byron. It was your mother's father's name.

Byron Erasmus Snipe. A wonderful man. He was the only man I respected more than myself. That's why we named you Byron.

BYRON: Well, the rest of the guys think it's gooney.

MOTHER: Oh, they do, do they? Well, let's understand one thing around here right now. You are not answering to the name Gus, and we are not accepting phone calls for anyone with that name. Understand that once and for all. Your grandfather would turn over in his grave. (*Sniffing a little.*) Oh, Byron. He thought you were the most beautiful baby.

BYRON: But, Mom. That's all in the past. This is now.

FATHER: And what does that mean?

BYRON: Ah, Pop, you know what I mean.

FATHER: Pop will get you nowhere.

BYRON: Well, I guess I'll go out and talk to Agnes. (*Exits into kitchen.*)

SANDY: Given any thought to that two dollars, Mom?

MOTHER: No. I have not. You children are irresponsible and ungrateful.

SANDY: No, we're not, Mom. It really has been a rough financial week for me, and Byron, I mean Gus,—(*Stern look from Mother.*) —I mean, Byron does have a point.

FATHER: What do you mean, Sandra?

SANDY: Well, Byron is a sticky name. Oh, I better get dressed. (*Exits.*)

MOTHER (*beginning to sob*): It was my father's name.

FATHER: Come to think of it, Doris, didn't your father have a nickname?

MOTHER: Yes, he did. Mother always called him Boots.

FATHER: Maybe there's something to it then. Well, it's office time. Be a good girl now, and hold the fort till I get back. (*Crosses to her. Kisses her. Exits.*)

MOTHER: Good-bye, Arnold. (*Sits and thinks for a while. With determination, she rises and crosses to kitchen door Down Left.*) Byron! Byron! (*Waits. Taps foot.*) Byron! O . . . h! (*Finally— desperately.*) GUS!!

Curtain

Once in a Blue Moon

OR

Moonstone Magic

CHARACTERS

MILLICENT
DIANA
ORKO
VOCK
MOON KING
MOON QUEEN

TIME: *A pleasant summer afternoon.*

PLACE: MILLICENT's *front porch.*

DIANA (*appearing suddenly*): Millicent! Hi! What are you doing?

MILLICENT: Oh, hi, Diana. Just reading. Come on up. What's new?

DIANA: I just came over to show you a present I got for my birthday. (*Holds out her hand with a ring.*) What do you think of it? It just came this morning.

MILLICENT: It's beautiful. Just beautiful! Is it your birthstone?

DIANA: Yes, it's a moonstone. Tomorrow is my birthday, June twenty-fifth.

MILLICENT: I love it. You know, it looks like the moon.

DIANA: Yes, that's why it's so whitish and cloudy. It's supposed to contain an image of the moon. Aunt Edna sent it to me with a note inside that said, "Have a very happy birthday, Di, but be careful of your moonstone. There's a legend that says, 'Whoever on her third finger gives it one good twist will live to see adventure she never knew exist.'"

MILLICENT (*laughing*): Wow! That's what I call superstition. Where did she get the ring?

DIANA: It's from New Mexico. Aunt Edna and Uncle Henry live in New Mexico. It was made by the Indians there. Aunt Edna said the Indians believe that this moonstone was washed up on the shore when the sun and the moon reached a position in relation to each other, which occurs about once every twenty-one years. That's where we get the expression 'Once in a blue moon.' Did you ever hear it?

MILLICENT: Yes, I think I've heard my mother use it every so often. Hey, why don't we try the ring? Why don't we see if it really has a charm connected with it? Have you twisted the ring on your finger yet?

DIANA: No. To tell the truth, I haven't really thought about it much. Anyway, I'm kind of afraid.

MILLICENT: Oh, come on. Let's try it. It's something to do. Nothing will probably happen anyway.

DIANA: Do you want to twist it on your finger?

MILLICENT: No. It wouldn't work for me. It's your ring.

DIANA: Well. Okay. Here goes! (*She twists the ring.*)

MILLICENT: Well.

DIANA: Well.

MILLICENT: Well—nothing. Oh, Diana. That's not your third finger! You mustn't count your thumb. Here. It's this one. (*She puts the ring on the right finger.*) Now try again.

DIANA: Okay. Here goes! (*Closes eyes. Stands completely still. Looks upward. We see her twist ring slowly.*) MILLICENT *has seated herself on a porch chair. She smiles, watching. Suddenly there is a noise. Lightning, thunder, blackout. All is darkness. As the lights go on we find the girls blinking and stretching in a new place.*)

DIANA: Oh, my! My goodness! What has happened? What have I done?

MILLICENT (*sneezing*): Ker-choo! Where are we? Ker-choo! My, but it's dusty here. Just look at my feet.

DIANA (*looking down*): What thick dust! It's like dry snow. Where on earth are we?

(*Two men suddenly appear. They are laughing. Their dress is strange.*)

ORKO (*laughing*): Ha! Ha! Ha! Where on earth are you? That is really rich! What a joke! Do you really want to know?

VOCK: Can't you guess where you are?

DIANA: Who are you?

MILLICENT: Tell us where we are!

ORKO: Can't you guess? What does your science book teach you? Where *on earth* are we? Ha! Ha! Ha!

DIANA: I don't think you're very funny. What do you mean, what does my science book teach me?

VOCK: Well, what place do you learn about—besides your precious earth—that has lots of dust on it?

MILLICENT: Why, I know. I know! The moon! The moon! Right?

VOCK: Of course. I was wondering when you'd finally get around to it.

DIANA: But how did we get here?

ORKO: We brought you. What did you think would happen when you twisted a moonstone? Ha! Ha! Ha! Ha!

DIANA: You two certainly think we're funny, don't you? Who are you?

ORKO: We are moon men.

MILLICENT: Oh, the Man in the Moon.

VOCK: If you like, man in the moon—men in the moon. The same difference.

DIANA: Did we come in a space rocket?

VOCK: By Jupiter, no! We simply fastened our supersonic, gray listic beam gaze on you and you drifted up to us.

DIANA: I—I don't remember.

ORKO: I know. You don't remember, and you won't remember. Moonstruck people never do.

MILLICENT: Look over there, Diana. That white light coming toward us. What is it, moon men?

ORKO: That is our king and queen coming to welcome their visitors. As they approach, remember to bow to them.

DIANA: We will.

MOON KING: Greetings. Greetings, strangers, and welcome to the moon.

MOON QUEEN: We hope you like it here. What are your names? (*The girls curtsy.*)

DIANA: I am Diana, and this is my friend Millicent.

MOON QUEEN: What pretty names. Diana is my name, too, you know.

DIANA: Oh, really? What a coincidence!

MOON KING: You earth children have probably heard stories about the moon goddess, Diana, haven't you?

MILLICENT: Why, yes. Yes, I have. But I didn't know there was a moon king.

MOON KING: Well, I'm sometimes referred to as the Man in the Moon. I'm sure you've heard of me.

DIANA: Oh, we have. But what a surprise! I never thought I'd meet you so suddenly—like this!

MOON KING: My pleasure, my dears!

DIANA: Tell me, are there many things to do on the moon?

MOON QUEEN: Well, that depends, Diana. The moon is really a jumping-off place to other things, if you know what I mean. From the moon you can travel to almost any place in the universe, but we amuse ourselves here counting the stars, throwing shadows on the earth at night, collecting moonstones, and tossing them . . .

DIANA: Oh, my moonstone! I almost forgot. Is it still here on my finger? (*Looks to see.*) Yes. It's still here.

MOON QUEEN (*examining* DIANA's *ring*): What a beautiful stone! That's a particularly nice one! That's what I would call a good wishing stone.

MILLICENT: That's how we got here, you know.

MOON QUEEN: Yes, the boys told me. Now that you know how to get here, you must come more often.

MILLICENT: But the moon men said we won't remember.

MOON KING: That is true, but you will always have the desire to try it again, and we'll see a lot of you.

DIANA: I want to come again, but I think I'd better be getting back to earth again. I'm hungry. Dinner will be ready soon, and my mother will be wondering where I am.

MOON QUEEN: In that case, my dear, you'd best be going. When you come again, we will visit our satellite Yurkus and show you how we test our listic beam gaze.

MILLICENT: That sounds exciting. I hate to leave.

MOON KING: We understand, my dears. Vock and Orko, fasten your safety gaze.

VOCK AND ORKO: Yes, Majesty. (*They bow. Then they stand, the girls' profiles to them. They put both hands on their shoulders and gaze deeply into their eyes. The* KING *and* QUEEN *wave and leave. Lights dim. Thunder clap. We are back on the porch.* MILLICENT *is sitting on chair, smiling.* DIANA *is standing, facing front with eyes shut.*)

DIANA: Oh, Millicent, I forgot! How about if I come over after dinner and we try this again. We're eating early tonight, because my mom and dad want to meet my grandma's plane at seven P.M. Okay? I have to go now.

MILLICENT (*disappointed*): Oh, gee! Well, okay. I'll see you after dinner. I'll be waiting. Now don't forget. I have a feeling there's something to all this.

DIANA: Do you? Maybe there is, but I think it's just superstition. So long. See you later.

MILLICENT: So long. (DIANA *leaves.*) That's funny, but I have the feeling that a lot of electricity just went through me. I never had a feeling like this before.

Curtain